New

Off the Beaten Path™

"In our promotional campaign, we refer to New Hampshire as 'The road less traveled.' The Rogers take you down this road and many others in their quest to uncover the hidden treasures that make up the Granite State."
—Lauri E. Ostrander, Director
New Hampshire Office of Travel and Tourism Development

"The authors are a rarity in the world of guidebooks. In their introduction, Barbara Radcliffe Rogers and Stillman Rogers, both travel writers with global experience, talked about how delighted they were to write about their home state."
—James Heckman, Assistant Editor
WOODALL's Publications

Praise for earlier editions:

"A New Hampshire guidebook that will both entertain and inform New Hampshire natives and visitors alike. This book deserves a permanent home in the glove compartment of your car."
—The Honorable Walter Peterson, former governor of New Hampshire and past president of Franklin Pierce College

"Unusual places that are worth making a detour for."
—*The Boston Globe*

"Hidden treasures unknown to many New Hampshire nat'
—*Northeast Outdoors*

Help Us Keep This Guide Up to Date

Every effort has been made by the author and editors to make this guide as accurate and useful as possible. However, many things can change after a guide is published—establishments close, phone numbers change, facilities come under new management, etc.

We would love to hear from you concerning your experiences with this guide and how you feel it could be made better and be kept up to date. While we may not be able to respond to all comments and suggestions, we'll take them to heart and we'll also make certain to share them with the author. Please send your comments and suggestions to the following address:

The Globe Pequot Press
Reader Response/Editorial Department
P.O. Box 833
Old Saybrook, CT 06475

Or you may e-mail us at:

editorial@globe-pequot.com

Thanks for your input, and happy travels!

OFF THE BEATEN PATH™ SERIES

New Hampshire

THIRD EDITION

Off the Beaten Path™

Barbara Radcliffe Rogers
and Stillman Rogers

The Globe Pequot Press

Old Saybrook, Connecticut

Maps created by Equator Graphics © The Globe Pequot Press
Illustrations by Carole Drong
Cover and text design by Laura Augustine
Cover photo: Images© PhotoDisc, Inc.

Off the Beaten Path is a trademark of The Globe Pequot Press

Library of Congress Cataloging-in-Publication Data

Rogers, Barbara Radcliffe
    New Hampshire : off the beaten path / Barbara Radcliffe Rogers and
Stillman Rogers ; [illustrations by Carole Drong]. —3rd ed.
      p. cm. —(Off the beaten path series)
    Includes index.
    ISBN 0-7627-0193-5
    1. New Hampshire—Guidebooks. I. Rogers, Stillman, 1939– II. Title.
III. Series.
    F32.3.R64   1998
    917.4204'43—dc21   97-42259
                                                    CIP

Manufactured in the United States of America
Third Edition/First Printing

In loving memory of George Radcliffe and Norman Rogers, the fathers who chose New Hampshire as our childhood home, and of James C. Cleveland, who as a U.S. Congressman worked so long and hard to preserve its character and protect its land.

Acknowledgments

Any book is a joint effort, but this one has profited from the help of friends and family all over New Hampshire—and from a number of others who were strangers when we began, but are now counted as friends.

They have shared with us their favorite off the beaten path places, those restaurants, inns, hiking trails, and back roads that even a traveler used to poking into all the corners might miss. Our gratitude goes to Joan Farrel, Judy Hampe, Chris Hamm, Joanne Lemieux, Ted and Elsie Miner, Pauline and Frank Mooney, Lee Stark, Larry Pletcher, Nina Gardner, Dennis and Sandy Brennan, Kathleen Hatt, Philip Hollman, Mike and Merri Hern, Joe Keenan, Ray Gorman, Betty Falton, Käthe Dillman, Art and Nancy Brennan, Doris Thibeault, Liz and Dennis Hagar, Michael Coyle, David Emerson, Niels Nielsen, and Susan and Malcolm McLane.

Very special thanks go to Len Reed of Bethlehem for the hours he spent telling us about places we would never have found without him. It was Len who also suggested many of the wonderful inns that welcomed us after long days of travel, and which we, in turn, recommend in this book. Many more were suggested by Dick Hamilton, from his vast knowledge of the White Mountains that he so readily shared with us.

We have shared our travels over the years with many friends: hikes and backroads with Patty Hanson, mountain trails and fishing boats with Carole Belsky and John Norton, campfires with Fred and Sta Gursky, campsites with Mark and Marge Davis, and miles of trails above the timberline with Howard and Sue Poore.

ACKNOWLEDGMENTS

Possibly the most hilarious of these adventures we have shared with Frank and Maria Sibley, as we searched for gorges, boulders, and ghost towns. Julie and Lura have always been fun to travel with, whether we were slipping over rocky trails in search of a waterfall in a downpour of rain, or enjoying a leisurely second cup of tea at a Portsmouth bakery.

Our fondest appreciation goes to Dee Radcliffe, who has explored every corner of the state and whose notes and suggestions led us to places even the locals didn't know about. Her good humor and enthusiasm will always place her among life's best traveling companions.

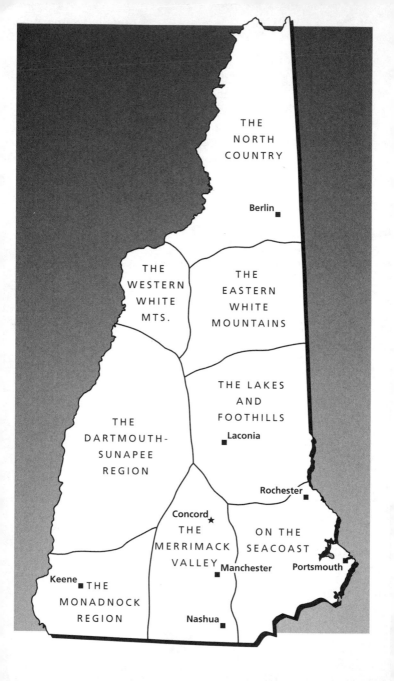

THE
NORTH
COUNTRY

Berlin ■

THE
WESTERN
WHITE
MTS.

THE
EASTERN
WHITE
MOUNTAINS

THE LAKES
AND
FOOTHILLS

THE
DARTMOUTH-
SUNAPEE
REGION

■ Laconia

Rochester ■

Concord ★

ON THE
SEACOAST

THE
MERRIMACK
VALLEY

Manchester ■

Portsmouth

Keene ■ THE
MONADNOCK
REGION

Nashua ■

Contents

Introduction

How do you introduce a friend, one with whom you've shared many of life's pleasures, one whose company never fails you? What can you possibly say of your friend that will capture those qualities that are most endearing and most enduring?

New Hampshire is that friend to us. The first memories of our childhoods are set here. The first ocean waves we played in broke on New Hampshire beaches; the first mountains we climbed, slopes and trails we skied—they were New Hampshire's. We've lived and traveled in many other parts of the world, but when asked a few days ago which of all the places that we've traveled is our favorite, we said in unison, and without second thought, New Hampshire.

The tremendous diversity of New Hampshire's landscapes makes it visually exciting and also provides a wide variety of activities, particularly for those who enjoy the outdoors. The challenges of its terrain, soil, and climate have given its people a unique character—or perhaps such a place has always attracted those of independent and self-sufficient spirit.

New Hampshire people do tend to be an independent lot; most of them say exactly what they think. Another disconcerting trait to those who don't know us well is that you can't always tell about us by our looks. The size of a person's fortune often bears no relation to the size of one's home or the make of one's car. It is often said of Boston ladies that they don't buy their hats; they have them. New Hampshire people are like that too. The beautiful farmhouse may be all that's left several generations later and may be kept up by a lot of hard work alone; the tiny cottage with the gate askew may be the home of a millionaire. We tend to live in what we have.

The same trait is true of restaurants, which is very confusing to the traveler used to decorator interiors and flashy exteriors. You can't always judge a restaurant by its cover, and very often the plainest place or the most staid of inns may have a chef who retired to the country from a four-star bastion of haute cuisine. Surprises are what New Hampshire is full of, and they make each day a happy adventure.

You Can't Get There from Here

*A*s a rule of thumb, you can get north and south, but not east and west on public buses. The main routes run from Boston to Montreal or Portland, Maine, passing through Portsmouth, Concord, Keene, Manchester, Nashua, and a few other cities farther north. But you can't get from Portsmouth to Keene without going back to Boston. The major bus lines are Vermont Transit (800–451–3292), Concord Trailways (800–639–3317), and Greyhound (603–436–0163). You can fly into the modern Manchester Airport, served by a variety of airlines, and to Keene, Portsmouth, and Lebanon, each served by a single carrier.

"Off the beaten path" is a relative thing. By most standards, the whole state is off the beaten path. There are only three areas that are congested by traffic even in the height of tourist season. If lodging is heavily booked during the most popular weeks, it is not because there are too many people here, but because resorts do not line our roads. Reservations are always a good idea during July and August and around the first week of October. Places such as Garfield Falls, which even many local people have not seen, require travel on unpaved roads. But none of these require four-wheel-drive vehicles, except in winter or early spring when some roads are muddy or not plowed.

If You Don't Like it, Wait a Minute

*M*ark Twain (and just about everyone else) had some choice words about the "infinite variety" of New England weather. Most of the exaggerated stories you've heard are probably true. Average temperatures don't tell you much. One day it may be sunny and 80 degrees, the next day may be 50 degrees and raining, but the average temperature for the period will be calculated at 65, although neither day **was** 65. And, the 24-hour averages don't tell you what the daytime temperature was. That in mind, you may find the following "official" average temperatures remotely helpful: Jan., 21 degrees Fahrenheit; Feb., 23 degrees Fahrenheit; Mar., 32 degrees Fahrenheit; Apr., 44 degrees Fahrenheit; May, 56 degrees Fahrenheit; June, 65 degrees Fahrenheit; July, 70 degrees Fahrenheit; Aug., 67 degrees Fahrenheit; Sept., 60 degrees Fahrenheit; Oct., 49 degrees Fahrenheit; Nov., 38 degrees Fahrenheit; and Dec., 25 degrees Fahrenheit. In reality, expect most summer days to be in the 70s, spring and fall in the 50s and 60s, winter in the 20s and 30s. Humidity tends to be high year-round, which makes the cold seem colder and the hot seem hotter. The nice thing, as Mark Twain suggests, is that it never stays any way for very long. In general, the best weather tends to be in August, September, and October, with less rain than in the spring, and fewer hot, humid days than earlier in the summer. The worst cold spells usually come in December and January. November is gray and March muddy, but with some glorious days.

Which brings us to the question of when to come. New Hampshire is a seasonal state, and each month has its attractions. The best time for you to explore the Granite State depends upon your tastes and interests. Winter is glorious, filled with crystal-cold days for skiing or snowshoeing across white meadows with clear views of mountains through leafless trees. Night brings the stars so close you can spot constellations you never saw before and is a good time for a sleigh ride and a blazing fire in the hearth. Snow covers all the hardscrabble farms and rock-filled fields, and the air is clear and smells of wood smoke. But if you like little museums or want to hike to waterfalls, winter is not the best season.

Spring is good for country walks and hikes. Sugar houses come briefly to life, shrouded in steam and smelling of sweet maple syrup. With the end of the sap run, spring wildflowers carpet the woodlands, and the view of the mountains is softened, but not obscured, by leaves the size of mouse ears. Spring peepers fill the evening air with chirping, and strawberry farms invite you to pick your own. A lot of the little places aren't open yet, but people in the ones that are have time to chat and tell you about local places. Bed and breakfast hosts have time to share a glass of sherry with you after dinner. Spring comes so fast that you can almost watch the apple blossoms unfold.

Summer is full of festivals celebrating almost everything from blueberries to zucchinis, and every little town has its historical society open. Days are long and not too hot to enjoy hikes and climbs. Lake shores and mountain brooks offer swimming.

After Labor Day, the weather is still summery, but there is a lull in the number of tourists until the end of the month. Farmers' markets are filled with produce and jars of glistening jellies. Hiking is at its very best, and the roadsides are brightened by patches of turning swamp maples.

Foliage paints the state, from north to south, in brilliant shades of red and gold. It begins in mid-September in the north country and lasts until mid- to late October in the Monadnock region. The peak can vary by a week or so, depending on the weather, but any area will have at least two weeks of good color, usually more.

What's Going on Here?

*T*he major cities have daily newspapers, and every area has its free weekly paper listing local events, festivals, church suppers, and just about everything else. The daily papers have special sections, usually late in the week, with entertainment and events calendars for the coming week. Many papers also print special summer sections, which are available free at information centers early in the summer. The major newspapers are the Union Leader and New Hampshire Sunday News (Manchester), Keene Sentinel, Foster's Daily Democrat (Dover), The Portsmouth Herald, Concord Monitor, Claremont Eagle, Valley News (Lebanon), Nashua Telegraph, Laconia Citizen, News and Sentinel (Colebrook), and Coos County Democrat (the north country).

So plan your travel dates according to your own interests, or better yet, come often and enjoy the best of each season.

Prices are a tricky thing to provide in a guide book, but we have done it anyway. They change with economic conditions, even seasons and weather conditions, since restaurants depend upon the markets for fresh produce and seafood. Lodging rates usually rise during the busiest times and drop during the slower ones. We have given dollar amounts when they seemed fairly likely to remain constant and elsewhere have used general ranges. For bed and breakfast places we consider $60 to $70 a night for two people to be moderate; for inns and hotels without breakfast, $70 to $85 is moderate. In restaurants, $10 to $20 is moderate for the main course, and we've further broken that into a high and low if the prices fall into a close range. How you add to that with other courses and wine will affect your bill, of course, but the entrée price sets the base. Sometimes we've been even more specific, especially if the prices are exceptional.

Now to all the usual disclaimers, the caveat emptor endemic to travel guides: Things change, especially in the restaurant business. We've tried to choose places with consistent ownership, but when we discover a great new spot, we can't wait five years to share it with you. If you find our recommendations not up to our descriptions, there are several possible reasons. The restaurant in question may have changed owners or chefs, or it may have just plain gone downhill. Your taste in food may not be the same as ours. One man's pâté is another's "ptoooi," as Confucius wisely observed. There is no substitute for your own good judgment. If you get inside and don't think it's the right place for you, leave. In those memorable cases where a place we've recommended doesn't look like what it tastes like, we've mentioned that fact so that you will expect it. If in doubt, don't be embarrassed to ask to see a menu before you're seated. New Hampshire people don't buy pigs in a poke and they don't expect you to either.

Enjoy New Hampshire as we do. We think that you'll agree after you've met the state in person that it's a place where familiarity breeds both respect and love.

To Find Out More

*W*rite or call the New Hampshire Office of Travel and Tourism, P.O. Box 856, Concord, NH 03302; (800) 386–4664 to order a copy of "The Official New Hampshire Guidebook," a handy compilation of advertising and listings. To speak to a live voice, call (603) 271–2343. The state's Web site at www.visitnh.gov gives general information on events, weather, and attractions. For an update on fall foliage conditions call (800) 258–3608, and for alpine ski conditions call (800) 258–3608. Cross country conditions are at (800) 262–6660. For a listing of private campgrounds call (800) 822–6764 or (603) 846–5511.

White Mountains Attractions, North Woodstock 03262; (800) 346–3687 or (603) 745–8720, can send you information on the northern part of the state, as will the Mt. Washington Valley Chamber of Commerce, North Conway 03860; (800) 367–3364. The Seacoast Council on Tourism, Portsmouth 03801; (800) 647–3296 or (603) 436–9800, will send material on the southeastern corner of the state.

The prices and rates listed in this guidebook were confirmed at press time. We recommend, however, that you call establishments to obtain current information before traveling.

On the Seacoast

New Hampshire has the shortest seacoast of any coastal state—only 18 miles long—but it's also one of the most historic. The first European settlers established a settlement at Odiorne Point in 1623, and later the same year a fishing village was established at Dover Point on the northern banks of the Piscataqua River on Little Bay. The Odiorne Point settlement was abandoned, but the Dover settlers built a meetinghouse and homes, which became the first permanent settlement in the colony.

The histories of this area, the American colonies, and the young nation are inextricably intertwined. The first American flag to be saluted by a foreign power flew from the mast of the *Ranger,* which sailed from Portsmouth in 1777. The flag was sewn by Portsmouth ladies of fabric cut from their dresses. Portsmouth today, for all of its funky shops and bright eateries, still has the air of a prosperous eighteenth-century seaport.

Exeter, too, was a shipbuilding town and a lively port. Although it has now lost its navigable link with the sea, its fine buildings still speak of the profitable India trade. Inland from the shores of the Great Bay stretched almost unbroken farmland, and, although more heavily settled than other parts of the state, the area is still rich in farms and orchards.

On the Seacoast

ROCHESTER

SOMERSWORTH

COCHECO TOWN

202

16

4

DOVER

108

PORTS AND FORTS

DURHAM

GREAT BAY

125

Great Bay

PORTSMOUTH

RAYMOND

101

THE PONDS

102

EXETER

SOUTH COAST

95

1

HAMPTON

108

DERRY

93

125

NEW HAMPSHIRE
MASSACHUSETTS

111

SALEM

N

0   10 mi
0   10 km

THE SEACOAST'S TOP PICKS

Fort Constitution

Great Island Common

Fort Stark

Odiorne Point

Drisco House

The Abbott Grocery Store

Port of Portsmouth Maritime Museum

Wentworth-Coolidge Mansion

Urban Forestry Center

Isles of Shoals

Whale watches

Little Boar's Head

Fuller Gardens

Tuck Museum

The Science and Nature Center

Gilman Garrison House

American Independence Museum

Piscataqua River Cruises

The Little Bay Buffalo Company

Great Bay Estuarine Research Reserve

Emery Farm

Woodman Institute

Point of View Farm

Harlow's Bread and Cracker Company

Pawtuckaway Boulders

Sandown Depot Railroad Museum

Sandown Meeting House

Although most visitors' view of the New Hampshire coast is the traffic and commercialism of Route 1, there are lovely and quiet back roads to enjoy even in this playground area. Portsmouth, too, has its surprises, tucked away amid its tangle of old lanes and paths that grew into streets. New Hampshire, as a colony, began in this seacoast area, and it's an appropriate place for us to begin exploring the state.

Portsmouth and the seacoast are accessible by air and bus, but if you are taking a bus, make sure it stops at Market Square, downtown. Some of the buses use the Pease International Tradeport, out of town, and there is no bus service to the city, so if you arrive by air or your bus lets you off there, you'll have to call a cab. This is an odd gap in otherwise excellent public transportation.

You can travel throughout the seacoast area from Hampton through Portsmouth to Rochester and as far west as Exeter on the **Coast** transportation system. Its seven routes provide bus service from the Massachusetts border, all along the ocean and up the Maine border to Farmington and to all of the towns along Great Bay. Fares are between $.75 and $2.00; exact change is required, so bring a supply of ones and quarters. Half-fare for seniors (65) and disabled is between 9:30 A.M. and 2:30 P.M. A complete fare and route guide is available at the Portsmouth Chamber of Commerce, town and city town halls, local businesses and on the buses, or call (603) 862–1931. For specific route or fares questions you can also call (603) 862–2328 from 6:30 A.M. to 10:30 P.M. Monday–Friday or 8:00 A.M. to 9:30 P.M. on Saturday.

AUTHORS' FAVORITE ATTRACTIONS/EVENTS ON THE SEACOAST

Strawbery Banke, Portsmouth (603) 433–1100

Whale Watching:

Great Bay Cruises, Portsmouth (603) 431–5500

New Hampshire Seacoast Cruises, Rye (603) 964–5545

Atlantic Fishing Fleet, Rye (603) 964–5220

The Portsmouth Harbour Trail, Portsmouth (603) 436–1118

Odiorne Point State Park, Rye (603) 436–8043

Hampton Beach, Hampton (800) GET–A–TAN

Market Square Day, mid-June, Portsmouth (603) 436–1118

Jazz Weekend and Festival, late June, Portsmouth (603) 436–7678

Prescott Park Arts Festival, July-August, Portsmouth (603) 436–1034

Seafood Festival and Sidewalk Sale, early September, Hampton Beach (603) 926–8717

Strawbery Banke Candlelight Stroll, early December, Portsmouth (603) 433–1100

Seacoast Trolley Company has trolley service around Portsmouth and to Wallis Sands State Beach, Odiorne Point State Park, Rye Beach, New Castle Common and Strawbery Banke, and just about every place we mention in this section. Daily service is available from mid-June to Labor Day, 10:00 A.M. to 6 P.M. Sunday–Thursday and until 8:00 P.M. on Friday and Saturday. It leaves Market Square on the hour, Strawbery Banke at 47 minutes past the hour and other locations on a schedule, which is available at tourist information offices and on the trolley. There is no phone to call. Fares are $2.00 to $4.00 (for the 1 hour narrated tour), and reboarding is free with the tour ticket.

Lighthouse at Fort Constitution

Ports and Forts

The link with the sea did not end with the sailing of the last clipper. Ships were built in Portsmouth for both world wars, and the forts that guarded the harbor in the Revolution still dot the coast.

New Castle, once called Great Island, was the first seat of government and even now looks like the tiny prosperous fishing and seafaring village of its colonial origins. Streets too narrow for sidewalks are lined with houses whose doorways open directly onto the roadway. The numbers on them are not addresses, but dates, most of them from the 1600s and 1700s.

Fort Constitution had its beginning in 1632 with the earthworks and four "great guns"; a blockhouse was

6

built in 1666, and at the end of the century a breastwork was built to protect the military stores. It was named Fort William and Mary.

Paul Revere, the Boston silversmith and patriot, is best known for his ride the night of April 18, 1775. But in New Hampshire, he's remembered for a ride almost four months earlier. On December 13, 1774, he brought a message that British troops were coming from Rhode Island to protect the garrison and secure it against the fractious Sons of Liberty. The next day, 400 Sons of Liberty converged on the fort and liberated one hundred barrels of gunpowder and some small arms, which they loaded on a gundalow (a type of boat built at Portsmouth and used to navigate tidal rivers) and sailed up the Oyster River to Durham. They hid the gunpowder in homes and under the pulpit of the meetinghouse until they could haul it by oxcart to Cambridge for use at Bunker Hill. On December 15, before the British could get reinforcements, another group helped themselves to sixteen small cannon and whatever other military supplies they could carry off. It was the first active engagement of the Revolution.

Renamed Fort Constitution, it was used in 1812 and every other war until it was returned to the state of New Hampshire in 1961. Its walls and ramparts are a fine place for viewing the lighthouse, harbor, and Fort McClary, which guards the other side of this harbor entrance from Kittery Point, Maine. Visitors must observe the parking restrictions posted at the Coast Guard Station entrance. Open 8:00 A.M. to 4:30 P.M. daily.

For access to the rocks and sandy beach of the neighboring shore, go through *Great Island Common,* a park overlooking the harbor. From here you can see two lighthouses, islands, and Fort Constitution, as well as passing sailboats. Rocky tidal areas surround the park with pools to explore and a gentler tide than the one that crashes against the rocks along the ocean. While the beach isn't very long, it's set in a very attractive cove. The park provides picnic tables, a pavilion, and grills, as well as playgrounds, ballfields, and restrooms. There are no camping facilities. Open daily May to September until dark; admission is $2.00 per adult; seniors and children are free.

Close to this park, look for the entrance to Wild Rose Lane, which ends at **Fort Stark.** It is another of the seven forts built to protect Portsmouth Harbor and the naval shipyard. Although it was the site of earthworks during the Revolution and the War of 1812 and of a later stone fort, the present batteries were built at the turn of the century and were used in both world wars. Be careful as you climb around the batteries; a flashlight will be handy if you plan to explore inside. Look for the tracks in the ceiling of Battery Hunter where ammunition was moved from the magazine and hoisted through a hole in the ceiling to the enormous guns in their emplacements above. The huge steel doors of the magazines stand ajar, grass grows from the cement, and one round gun emplacement has begun to slide down the crumbling cliff. Open Saturday and Sunday 10:00 A.M. to 5:00 P.M. between Memorial Day and Labor Day.

Facing New Castle Island and Fort Stark is **Odiorne Point,** where the first Europeans in the state settled. Site of Fort Dearborn during World War II, the grass-covered hills are actually camouflaged casemates for gun emplacements and their support systems. The entire point is now a nature center, with diverse coastal habitats to explore. Along with the rocky shore and salt marsh, there are a freshwater marsh and coastal woods. A drowned forest of pine, birch, and hemlock stumps is firmly rooted about two feet below tide level at the south end. Throughout the natural habitat you can see signs of human habitation as well. Stone walls of old farmlands and a colony of summer cottages cross the area, and you may see the hardy remnants of some of the formal gardens of the long-gone cottages. The only one of these now standing is the Seacoast Science Center. Programs and tours on such varied subjects as wild shore edibles, sea legends, coastal defenses, whales, marshes, and geology are conducted by the New Hampshire Audubon Society and the University of New Hampshire Marine Science Program. The center offers activities for children, including a day camp program. Open daily, mid-May to mid-October, 8:00 A.M. to 8:00 P.M. A small entry fee is charged. Write P.O. Box 674, Rye 03870 or call (603) 436–8043 (off-season 603–862–3460). For information on special programs call (603) 862–1088.

Hold Your Tongue

As "witches" were being burned in neighboring Massachusetts on no more than the testimony of children, Goody Walford of Portsmouth, described as an old crone and accused of witchcraft, brought a defamation suit against her accusers and was awarded damages by the court.

OFF THE BEATEN PATH

Portsmouth is a lively city with warrens of back streets to explore. The path to its abundant historic homes is part of *"The Portsmouth Harbour Trail."*

A full-color map and thirty-two page guide are available ($2.00) and provide a handy and excellent reference to historic buildings and sites and varied architectural styles along the way. Write or call Greater Portsmouth Chamber of Commerce, 500 Market Street, P.O. Box 239, Portsmouth 03802-0239, (603) 436–1118, or go to the visitors kiosk at Market Square during the summer.

Much of Portsmouth is best seen on foot, and the city has wisely provided a good parking garage right in the center of town on Hanover Street. It's very inexpensive and avoids the hassle of trying to find a legal space on the narrow streets of this ancient port town. It's just one block north of Market Square off Market Street.

The original name for the settlement here was **Strawbery Banke,** after the river banks red with the fruit in the late spring. A restoration preserving nearly four centuries of this old waterfront neighborhood, saved from demolition in the 1950s, now uses the name Strawbery Banke. Thirty of the thirty-five historic homes here stand on their original foundations. The unusual feature of the restoration is that instead of returning the neighborhood to any single period and showing what things looked like then, the buildings and their furnishings show the evolution of homes, gardens, shops, and daily life throughout the entire period of its existence.

The most dramatic example of this whole-history approach is at the **Drisco House,** built in 1795. The house changed with the times, and when it was acquired, one side of the duplex was a "frozen in time" 1950s apartment. It has been saved as it stood, but the other half of the house has been restored to its origins as the store and home of an eighteenth-century mid-level tradesman. This, too, is unusual, for the homes that are usually saved and restored are those of wealthy and prominent citizens—homes far more elegant and ornate than the Drisco House. This one building, with its 1795 and 1955 halves, spans the history of the Puddle Dock neighborhood in Portsmouth.

The process of discovery and restoration is a continuing one, and visitors are invited to share in it through a number of exhibits showing cutaway walls and structural details. The *Joshua Jackson and Sherburn houses* are dedicated entirely to old house archaeology, showing not only how the homes were built, but also how historians can detect the changes made over the centuries. To anyone restoring an older home, looking inside the mechanics of original and renovated construction is an invaluable lesson. To the more casual visitor, it's just plain interesting.

Portsmouth was a major shipyard during World War II, and life on the home front in a coastal city is illustrated at *The Abbott Grocery Store,* restored to its 1943 appearance and contents. The storekeeper's apartment next door and exhibits in the rear of the building all show how life on the homefront changed during the war.

For more than fifty years the family of a New Hampshire governor of the Civil War era lived in the *Goodwin Mansion,* and his wife's detailed and spirited diaries provide information that has made it possible to restore

Thanks, Gov

*R*oyal Governor John Wentworth unwittingly helped train and equip three regiments of New Hampshire soldiers for the Continental Army, which were ready from the first shots of the Revolution. Wentworth had vigorously supported these as a local militia to defend Portsmouth in case of attack from French or other enemies of the crown; all they had to do was change their name and march off to Bunker Hill. These three regiments fought in nearly every major encounter and were credited with an important role in winning the war.

not only the house but her remarkable gardens as well. At various times in the summer and fall, Victorian teas are served in these gardens.

In keeping with the museum's philosophy, its newest restoration tells the story of a Russian Jewish family that settled in Puddle Dock at the turn of the century. **Shapiro House** celebrates the lives of the family of Abraham and Shiva Shapiro and is restored to the 1910 period. From the kosher kitchen to the bedrooms on the second floor, and even to family treasures and a boarders' room on the third floor, this is an immersion in the immigrant experience and of adaptation to life in a new country. Holidays appropriate to the family are celebrated here.

Without major endowment, Strawbery Banke continues to grow as funds are available, usually from local donations or entry fees. It is exciting to watch the restorations take place, and each visit gives a dimension of being part of its progress. Even the gifts purchased at the **Dunaway Store,** the museum's shop, help fund the restoration. It's like giving twice when you do your Christmas shopping there.

Speaking of Christmas, on the first two weekends of December, the village opens for a *Candlelight Stroll.* Candles light the windows as you wander through the streets with costumed carolers and musicians. The houses are decorated for the holidays and offer free refreshments to visitors. Craftspeople are at work, and you can shop for gifts in their workshops or in the museum stores. Each year brings new features, and it's an occasion for local people to enjoy the uncrowded winter quiet of Strawbery Banke. The stroll takes place on four evenings only, from 4:30 to 8:30 P.M., and costs $8.00 for adults and $4.00 for children ages ten to sixteen (younger children are admitted free).

The restored buildings are open daily 10:00 A.M. to 5:00 P.M. from May 1 through October 31. A two-day admission pass is $10.00 for adults, $7.00 for ages six to seventeen, and free for children under age six. Write Strawbery Banke, Marcy Street, P.O. Box 300, Portsmouth 03802 or call (603) 433–1100.

Gardeners should stop at *Prescott Park* across the street to see the All America Show Garden, where each year's All America selections are grown. Show gardens such as this are located in different parts of the country to demonstrate which flowers perform best in various climates. Northerners who spot boxwood at Strawbery Banke may wonder how it grows in New Hampshire. The answer is that Portsmouth and a tiny coastal strip are in a different gardening zone from the rest of the state, due to the moderating effect of the sea. In addition to the garden, the park has an active marina and hosts almost daily activities throughout the summer. The *Prescott Park Arts Festival* in July and August offers twilight and Sunday brunch concerts, theater, art shows, and craft shows. On the Saturday of Memorial Day weekend (or the first Saturday in June) area restaurants compete in a *Chowderfest* at the park, and on the Saturday of Columbus Day weekend they meet again for a *Chili Cook-Off* at midday.

Another lively Portsmouth event is the annual *Market Square Day*, the second Saturday of June. Music, food booths, activities, art exhibits, and crafts shows all end with fireworks. The city is ablaze with color, balloons, and throngs of people having fun. A *Jazz Weekend and Festival* is the last weekend in June, with the Festival on Sunday. It features regional and local musicians in live performance at Harbour Place, near Memorial Bridge and at Strawbery Banke. For information on specifics of these or other activities such as *First Night,* call the Greater Portsmouth Chamber of Commerce (603) 436–1118.

Nearby *St. John's Church* on Chapel Street, just off Bow Street, is a masterpiece of colonial architecture with later *trompe l'oeil* painting decorating its galleried interior. The bell in the steeple, still used to summon worshippers each Sunday, was captured at the French fortress at Louisburg, Nova Scotia, in 1745, brought to Portsmouth, and presented to this church. The bell fell during a fire in 1806 and was recast by Paul Revere. The church silver was given by Queen Anne, and the Brattle organ, built in England in 1662, is a pure baroque organ of the sort J. S. Bach played, and the oldest operating pipe organ in America. E. Power Biggs made a recording on it for the 1976 bicentennial celebrations. The church also has a copy of the rare "Vinegar Bible." Royal Governor Benning Wentworth is buried in the adjacent churchyard. You can see all of these things with the help of a little brochure that you will find in the front of the church. We hope you'll leave a contribution for the building's upkeep and repair when you leave.

Built at the Portsmouth Naval Shipyard in 1953, the *Albacore*, now at the **Port of Portsmouth Maritime Museum,** never went to war. Her mission was an experimental one, as she was planned to be redesigned and adapted as the prototype for the submarine of the future. The teardrop hull design made her the fastest submarine ever put in the water. That and dive brakes, sonar systems, and other new theories tested onboard have become part of modern submarine design. The fascinating story of this experimental submarine and how its fifty-five-member crew lived in its 205-foot-by-27-foot confines during its nineteen years of commission is told during a ten-minute video and a half-hour tour of the vessel. Now sunk in a dry basin so you can see the entire hull, the USS *Albacore* looks a bit like a beached whale up close. It's the only one of its kind, so if the sea and its ships interest you at all, don't pass up the chance to see it. Open 9:30 A.M. to 5:30 P.M. every day; the last tour begins at 5:00 P.M. Adults $4.00, seniors $3.00, children ages seven to seventeen $2.00, families $10.00. You'll find the *Albacore* on the Market Street Extension, or Route 1 bypass, 600 Market Street, Portsmouth; (603) 436–3680.

For entertainment in Portsmouth you can't do better than **The Music Hall**. This nicely restored theater is run by a local nonprofit organization and offers current movies, classic and foreign films, live theater, and music. Touring groups such as The Acting Company perform here on a regular basis. It's at 28 Chestnut Street, Portsmouth 03801, (603) 436–2400, or call the 24-hour film line at (603) 436–9900. Movie admissions are $6.00 including a $1.00 preservation fee; live performance fees vary. You might also want to check the *Spotlight* section of the *Portsmouth Herald,* a weekly supplement to the paper that covers music, theater, and the visual arts throughout the seacoast area, with addresses and phone numbers of clubs.

Portsmouth has developed a reputation for some of the best dining in the state, with a range of styles to choose from. *Cafe Mediterraneo* was opened by escapees from Boston's North End. Tired of high rents, they now provide some of the best Italian food north of Boston. A full menu of pasta, fish, chicken, and veal dishes are well prepared and reasonably priced from $6.00 to $13.00, most under $10.00. Try the lobster ravioli. It's open daily, 11:30 A.M. to 10:30 P.M. at 152 Fleet Street; (603) 427–5563.

More formal, *Anthony Alberto's Ristorante Italiano* has a venturesome menu in an elegant basement setting with fine woods and etched glass. For example, try Salmone d'Oro, a lemon-and-dill-encrusted salmon with a puree of yellow peppers and tomatoes or Anatra con Pesche, breast of duck with a port wine and ginger reduction. Pastas and entrees range from $12 to $22. It's at 59 Penhallow Street; (603) 436–4000.

A totally different dining experience awaits at *Dunfey's Aboard the* John Wanamaker. This former Philadelphia tugboat is moored under Memorial Bridge near Strawbery Banke, with great views of the harbor. Gourmet dining aboard the last steam-operated tug in the United States includes Red Snapper with a Calamata and braised fennel tart, gingered catfish, or braised chicken with a wild mushroom ragout. The innovative cuisine is nicely set off by the wood and polished brass of the restored ship. Entrees run $16 to $24. Open for lunch and dinner daily from May through Columbus Day, dinner Tuesday–Saturday, Columbus Day through April. It's moored at 1 Harbor Place, Portsmouth; (603) 433-3111.

Kukula's Trattoria has Italian specialties and more. Lamb Osso Bucco is joined on the list by Golden Wyoming Trout and Shrimp Orechette. Prices are $10 to $22, most midrange. Lunch Wednesday–Saturday, dinner daily, at 10 Market Square; (603) 436-1600.

Lindbergh's Crossing is another fine dining option. Try the pepper-crusted salmon roulade, southern French-fried rabbit or perhaps the bistro steak sandwich with caramelized onion and Gruyère cheese. Entrees are $11 to $21. Open daily, for dinner only, at 29 Ceres Street; (603) 431-0887.

A bit less expensive, ***Blue Mermaid World Grill*** has interesting and nicely done entrees tending toward Southwestern, Caribbean and South American specialties, as well as innovative pizza, wood-grilled burgers, quesadillas, and pasta. There is a deck in the courtyard and, in good weather, entertainment outdoors. Entrees are $10 to $14. Open daily for lunch and dinner, it's on The Hill (opposite the downtown parking garage); (603) 427-BLUE.

Muddy River Smokehouse is what it says it is, serving baby back ribs, chili, smoked chicken, pan-blackened catfish, jerk chicken—you get the idea. This is also a hot local venue for live Blues, with frequent performances. Call or check their Web page, www.muddyriver.com. The restaurant's open every day, serving lunch and dinner, and the downstairs lounge is open Wednesday–Saturday evenings, at 21 Congress Street; (603) 430–9582.

For picnics or take-out sandwiches with panache, go to *Brewer, Cook & Baker,* 104 Congress Street; (603) 436–5918. They have basket specials for breakfast or lunch and great sandwiches at reasonable prices. If a kosher deli is more your style, try *Goldi's Deli* at 106 Penhallow Street; (603) 431–1178. It's east of Market Street between Daniel and Bow Streets. You can order take-out or stay in their upbeat cafe to eat your lox.

Ceres Bakery, at 51 Penhallow Street, bakes incomparable breads, cookies, tortes, and coffee cakes. Nowhere else will you find such generous slices of the last two served up for $1.00 to $1.50. Hearty thick soups are served with a slice of their daily bread, or you can choose quiches or salads. Lunch with dessert will be under $5.00. It opens at 5:30 A.M. for travelers who like to be on the road early (603–431–6518). Another choice for pastry and sandwiches is *Cafe Brioche,* 14 Market Square; (603) 430–9225.

Within walking distance from Strawbery Banke and most of the other attractions of Portsmouth, the *Bow Street Inn* occupies the top floor of a harborside building that once housed a brewery. Tastefully decorated rooms with queen-size brass beds frame views of the harbor; breakfast breads are homemade and the hospitable innkeepers take time to suggest restaurants, activities, and their own favorite corners of Portsmouth. The inn is at 121 Bow Street, Portsmouth 03801; call (603) 431–7760.

The *Oracle House Inn* is a four-room bed-and-breakfast accommodation right next door to Strawbery Banke and is as historic as the museum. Built in 1702 by a British naval officer, it housed the first daily newspaper in the colony. The house has been meticulously restored, right down to the colors of the woodwork. Two of the rooms have private bath (one with Jacuzzi) and two share. Rates are $99 (shared bath) to $139 (Jacuzzi) in the summer, including breakfast. It's at 38 Marcy Street, Portsmouth; (603) 433–8827.

Out of town, where the Little Harbor Road ends at the water's edge, is the *Wentworth-Coolidge Mansion.* It is one of the very few residences of a royal governor virtually unchanged since the Revolution. The governor lived well. The home that he built in 1750 was originally even larger and was the most elegant of its day. It was not only his residence, but the center of government as well. You can tour the original rooms and the Governor's Council Chamber, where he signed the charters for land grants and towns throughout New Hampshire and Vermont. The grounds, where you are welcome to picnic, are planted with the first lilacs brought to the New World. They are the state flower, and if you visit New Hampshire in May you will see them blooming in dooryards, gardens, and at the sites of long-deserted farms throughout the countryside. Although technically an "exotic" here, lilacs have a long history in the state and have been accepted as native. Open from 10:00 A.M. to 5:00 P.M. from Memorial Day to Labor Day. (Perhaps this is a good place to mention that Memorial Day in New Hampshire is still observed on May 30, not the nearest Monday.) The Wentworth-Coolidge Mansion is on Little Harbor Road, off Route 1A in Portsmouth (603–436–6607).

South of Portsmouth, not far from Route 1, is the 150-acre property of the *Urban Forestry Center.* A beautiful place to visit for its gardens, woodland, and salt marsh landscapes, it is also an attractive demonstration area whose purpose is not only to protect this piece of land, but to show others how they can protect and enhance their own property as well. Individuals, municipalities, developers, and conservation commissions all look to the center for inspiration and advice. Throughout the property are mailboxes where you will find extensive information on each project. Plant-by-plant descriptions are available at the perennial border, and a thorough booklet on herb culture and uses, prepared by Tanya Jackson (one of New England's leading herb experts), is free at the herb garden. The Center sponsors lectures, field trips, and programs on natural history, wildlife, gardening, and New Hampshire forests. Most of the programs are on Thursday evenings and cost a modest $2.00 admission.

A "Garden for the Senses," created especially for the visually and physically impaired, emphasizes plants selected for flavor, fragrance, color, and texture, with wide paths and raised beds for easy access. An arboretum contains examples of trees for street plantings, cold-hardy trees, and those with unusual and interesting flowers, bark, or leaves. Several plantations

Whodunit?

John and Maren Hontvet shared their cottage on Smuttynose, one of the Isles of Shoals, with John's brother, Maren's brother, and his beautiful wife Anethe, all freshly arrived from Norway. Maren's sister, Karen, was visiting. A friend, Louis Wagner, lived in Portsmouth and was jobless. Thus the scene is set for the night of March 5, 1873.

The three men from Smuttynose decided to spend the night in Portsmouth, and they mentioned this to Louis, whom they met there. From here, the story has two distinctly different versions. The accepted one, based more on contemporary public opinion and sentiment than on the actual trial and testimony, is that Louis rowed a stolen dory 10 miles out to the island and, in an attempt to rob the house, hacked Anethe and Karen to death with an axe while Maren managed to escape and hide all night in the rocks along the shore. She identified him as the murderer, he was caught, almost lynched by incited mobs, tried and hanged.

While popular opinion of the era would not accept the idea of a family woman committing murder, the trial evidence points to Maren as the villain and shows no evidence that Wagner was even on the island that night. But anyone who knew the truth was dead, and Maren and John moved to Portsmouth, without either brother or the pretty sister-in-law. Smuttynose is uninhabited today.

and trails as well as ample space for watching birds that live in the marsh and shore areas add to the Center's attractions. Free and open year-round, the trails are favorites of cross-country skiers and snowshoe hikers (no motorized recreational vehicles). Hours are 7:00 A.M. to dusk daily. The office is open 8:00 A.M. to 4:00 P.M.

Monday through Friday. The Center is at 45 Elwyn Road (off Lafayette Road) in Portsmouth; call (603) 431–6774 for more information.

Off the coast, shared with Maine, but with access from New Hampshire, and visible only in clear weather, are the **Isles of Shoals.** Described by the writer and poet Celia Thaxter, who grew up there, they were painted by the impressionist artist Childe Hassam, who came to the summer arts colony that developed there. His work includes over 400 paintings of the islands, many of which were done to illustrate Thaxter's *An Island Garden,* a classic of garden writing as fresh in its facsimile reprint as it was at its original printing at the turn of the century. These islands are as wrapped in tales of shipwrecks, pirates, ghosts, and buried treasure as they are in fog. Craggy and barren as they were when Captain John Smith called them "barren piles of rock," the islands still fascinate visitors. The Isles of Shoals Steamship Company at 315 Market Street will take passengers to Star Island for a three-hour shore visit. Write them at P.O. Box 311, Portsmouth 03801 or call (603) 431–5500. Whale watching, fishing, harbor, and Great Bay cruises from Portsmouth are also offered by Portsmouth Harbor Cruises at Ceres Street Dock, 64 Ceres Street, Portsmouth 03801 (603–436–8084 or 800–776–0915). You can also take cruises there from Rye Harbor (see next section).

The South Coast

The shoreline in Rye is less developed than elsewhere, with long stretches of open salt marsh (some of it a wildlife preserve), and rocky coast broken by beaches. *New Hampshire Seacoast Cruises* operates boat trips from Rye Harbor including day and evening *whale watches* and two-hour *cruises to the Isles of Shoals.* For information write to them at P.O. Box 232, Rye 03870 or call (603) 964–5545. *Atlantic Fishing Fleet* offers deep-sea fishing trips and whale watches on board *Atlantic Queen II* from April through mid-October. For a schedule write to P.O. Box 678, Rye Harbor 03870 or telephone (603) 964–5220.

Island Cruises operates tours to the Isles of Shoals and Lobster Tours from Rye Harbor. The two-hour island tour is narrated with historical fact and tales of mysterious doings. On the one-hour lobster tour you learn all about the elusive crustacean and how they are harvested, coming face to face with one when a trap is brought aboard. During July and August, they operate the Island Tour at noon and 2:30 P.M. every day and 5:00 P.M. Thursday–Sunday, and the Lobster tour Saturday–Wednesday at 10:00 A.M. In June and September, they operate weekends only. Fares are $9 and $11 for adults. Contact them at P.O. Box 66, Rye 03870; (603) 964-6446.

Overlooking the ocean is *Saunders at Rye Harbor,* a local institution for more than seventy years. The menu offers a wider range of dishes than you would expect in a restaurant best known for its lobster. Seafood-stuffed mushroom caps, herbed toasted pita points, Jamaican scampi and five "healthy choices," including chicken Marsala, highlight the menu. On Route 1A; call (603) 964-6466.

For a shorebound excursion that gives you nature on one side and human nature on the other, walk or bicycle around *Little Boar's Head.* A 2-mile path goes along the ridge of a rocky promontory, with waves crashing on the rocks below. Inland stands a row of beach "cottages" built in the pre-income tax days when wealthy city dwellers moved their families and household staffs to the shore for the summer. In the early summer wild roses bloom along the path.

Roses at *Fuller Gardens* are clearly not wild: 1,500 carefully tended rosebushes thrive in the sea air in an All America Rose Display Garden, once part of a fine old Boar's Head estate. Both roses and perennial beds are at their peak in June, but the gardens are filled with blooms all summer and late into the fall. Don't miss the gate in the hedge leading to the cool, cedar-shaded Japanese garden with its pool, bridge, and stone lantern. Marble walkways surround a terraced formal garden. Open 10:00 A.M. to 6:00 P.M. daily during blooming season, the gardens are on Willow Avenue, which leaves Route 1A just north of its intersection with Route 101D, in North Hampton. The telephone is (603) 964–5414. Admission is $3.50.

The town of Hampton lies inland, out of hearing distance of raucous Hampton Beach. Follow Park Avenue east from Route 1 to find the original settlement at Meetinghouse Green. The old common is now a memorial park to the first settlers, with a stone for each of the pioneer families put there by their descendants. Across the street is the *Tuck Museum,* operated by the Hampton Historical Society, a group of buildings that includes an old one-room schoolhouse, a museum of early farm implements, the Seacoast Fire Museum, and a variety of exhibits on the area's history. It isn't the Smithsonian but it is a very approachable collection;

Fuller Gardens

most items are not in glass cases but right where you can see them. A playground on the shady lawn outside will amuse the children if your attention span exceeds theirs. Open 1:00 to 4:00 P.M. Thursday through Sunday from mid-June to mid-September. Admission is free. The museum is at 40 Park Avenue, Hampton 03842; call (603) 929–0781 for news of special events.

The Science and Nature Center at Seabrook Station, the area's power station, explores the various sources of energy and their effects on the environment. Hands-on exhibits, such as a bicycle-powered generator (how long can you keep the light burning?) and computerized quizzes, fill the science center, and an aquarium shows local marine life. The Oascoag nature trail winds through woods and marshlands where markers explain the habitats, natural history, and plant life. Shorebirds abound, and muskrats, foxes, rabbits, and woodchucks may wander within sight if you are quiet. Such salt marshes are important sources of food and breeding grounds for wildlife, as well as providing filtration areas to keep groundwater pure. Open Monday–Saturday in July and August, Monday–Friday the rest of the year; free admission. Write Seabrook Station, Route 1, Seabrook 03874 or call (603) 474–9521 or (800) 338–7482.

If you're staying in the area with children, they'll enjoy the petting farm at the Best Western *Seabrook Inn.* There's quite an assortment: rabbits and sheep, white doves and llamas, even a cow the kids can learn to milk and a pony to ride. The inn is at 9 Stard Road, Seabrook 03874; telephone (603) 474–3078.

Exeter, like Portsmouth, is a nice place for walking. Fine homes line its streets, and three of the finest Federal mansions face the bandstand in the center of town. The *Gilman Garrison House* was built of massive hewn logs in the late 1600s as a fortified garrison. In the mid-1700s the house was enlarged and remodeled, adding a wing and more formal rooms in which its owner felt more comfortable entertaining John Wentworth, the royal governor, during his visits to Exeter. These visits ended abruptly when the governor had to take refuge in Fort William and Mary and finally flee altogether at the outbreak of the Revolution. (Since Portsmouth was considered a hotbed of Toryism, the seat of the state's government moved to Exeter—making it the state's first capital.) Later, Daniel Webster boarded in this house while he was a student at Phillips Exeter Academy. Open June 1 to October 1, Tuesday, Thursday, Saturday, and Sunday, noon to 5:00 P.M. The Gilman Garrison House is at the corner of Water and Clifford streets in Exeter; call (603) 436-3205.

Also in the center of town is the *American Independence Museum,* a newly established combination of the Ladd-Gilman House (home of New Hampshire's governor during the Revolution) and the Folsom Tavern, with the archives of the Society of the Cincinnati. The collections in the two eighteenth-century buildings feature furnishings from the 1600s, two annotated drafts of the U.S. Constitution, and historic artifacts. Escorted tours are given Wednesday through Sunday afternoons (the last tour begins at 4:00 P.M.), May through October. Located at One Governor's Lane (off Center Street), Exeter 03833; telephone (603) 772-0861.

Art Deco enthusiasts should stop at the *Ioka Theater* in downtown Exeter, where the lobby has been restored to its 1915 origins and the soda fountain serves floats and phosphates. Classic films are a specialty here. This is also a venue for live performances; call for a schedule. The soda fountain is open 11:00 A.M. to 5:30 P.M. daily (603-772-2222).

Known best to students, parents, and alumni of Phillips Exeter Academy, *The Inn of Exeter* offers a wide variety of rooms that retain the charm of a historic hotel while providing modern and stylish lodgings. Antiques accent the spacious lobby, which sets the hotel's tone of unstuffy elegance. The dining room scores high, even in the seacoast area's abundance of good restaurants. Favorite entrées are given new life with carefully chosen accompaniments—tournedos of beef paired with apricots and pistachios, for example—and each dish is prepared with meticulous attention to detail. The restaurant is busy during special events at the Academy, so call ahead to be sure of a table. The inn is at the corner of Front and Pine streets, Exeter 03833; telephone (603) 772–5901 or (800) 782–8444.

Great Bay and Cocheco Town

Past Portsmouth harbor, the Piscataqua River opens into Little Bay, which is fed by the Oyster River and **Great Bay.** At 5 miles long, Great Bay is the largest inland body of salt water in New England, but it's very hard to see since only one road, Route 4, passes within sight. Even that allows views of only the northern end. The towns that lie along the rivers feeding it are all far from its tidal shores.

The best way to see this area is from the water, on a **Piscataqua River cruise,** a three-hour trip from Portsmouth to Durham, with a stop at the site of the Bickford Garrison to learn how it was defended in 1694 by one farmer who cleverly changed coats and voices to make the post seem well-manned. The tour includes a buffalo farm (see below) and a chance to sample a buffalo burger as well. Offered on weekends in the fall, when the foliage along the wooded shores is at its best, cruises are run by Isles of Shoals Steamship Co., 315 Market Street, P.O. Box 311, Portsmouth 03802; telephone (603) 431–5500 or (800) 894–5509 in New Hampshire, (800) 441–4620 outside the state.

The Little Bay Buffalo Company is a family-run farm on rolling meadows and woodlands extending to the waters of Little Bay. It is habitat for a number of wildlife species and a migratory stop for waterfowl. The bison here are not for petting; they are usually visible in the pasture, often at close range. Also at the farm are displays on the interrelationship between the bison and the Indians' way of life, as well as information on local Indians who camped here in the summer to fish and hunt. A Company Store sells buffalo meat, hides, and related products such as buffalo tooth necklaces. The clear message here, well stated by the Langley family, is that using resources requires responsibility. To reach the farm, take Durham Point Road from Route 108 and watch for the small sign on Langley Road to the left. Open daily mid-April through late November, 9:00 A.M. to 5:00 P.M.; observation area open until sunset. 50 Langley Road, Durham 03824; telephone (603) 868–3300.

Durham is best known for the *University of New Hampshire,* which dominates the town and brings it to life. Beside Thompson Hall on the campus is a lovely ravine filled in May with lilacs of every shade from white to dark purple.

Off Durham Point Road, on the way to Newmarket, is the *Great Bay Estuarine Research Reserve,* more than 4,000 acres of tidal waters, mud flats, salt marsh, tidal creek woodlands, fields, and meadows on Adams Point. There is no nature center or organized visitor program here, but the habitat is filled with the flora and fauna peculiar to tidal estuaries. A boat put-in and parking area are reached by a stone-wall-bordered road that ends at the Jackson Laboratory, an estuarine research center. Park there to reach the viewing platform (handicapped accessible) overlooking rolling meadows with the bay in the background. The air is filled with the trill of birds. For information on the Great Bay Reserve, call (603) 868–1095.

Emery Farm was established in 1655, which, eleven generations later, makes it high on the list of the nation's oldest family farms. Here you can pick your own strawberries, blueberries, or raspberries. Juicy tree-ripened peaches and garden produce as well as local maple syrup, honey, and fresh home-baked breads are sold; New Hampshire crafts and pottery add to the unique farmstand. In the spring they sell herb plants and garden flats from their greenhouse. The farm is open every day, Easter through Christmas Eve (they also sell Christmas trees) from 9:00 A.M. to 6:00 P.M. Emery Farm is on Route 4, 2 miles east of Durham (603–742–8495).

Dover was the scene of repeated Indian attacks during the early years of the settlement, so nearly all of its garrison houses were destroyed. The only one still surviving is the 1765 *Damm Garrison,* which is protected by a roofed lattice portico between two brick buildings of the *Woodman Institute.* In original condition, this heavy log structure houses a collection of early furnishings and implements. The two exhibition buildings of the Woodman Institute are a tribute to the inquiring minds of the Victorians who assembled their contents. The collection of mounted animals contains specimens of most of the mammals native to the state and many, such as an 8-foot-tall polar bear, that are not. In addition to an extensive collection of rocks, minerals, and lepidoptera, the museum displays fine examples of Sioux beadwork. President Lincoln's saddle, used in his last review of troops and inherited by his aide Colonel Daniel Hall after the assassination, highlights the Civil War collection on the third floor. The Hale House contains fine antique furniture and a variety of collections from the nineteenth century. Open Tuesday through Saturday, 2:00 to 5:00 P.M., at The Woodman Institute, 182 Central Avenue, Dover 03820; call (603) 742–1038.

Salmon Falls Stoneware is a potters' studio where they make salt-glazed stoneware and decorate it by hand with traditional designs. It is open daily, 9:00 A.M. to 5:00 P.M. You can find Salmon Falls Stoneware in the old Boston and Maine Engine House on Oak Street in Dover (603–749–1467).

Dover is a good place to use as a base while visiting the seacoast area. Quieter than Portsmouth or the beach towns, it is easier to find lodging here, especially in the summer. *Highland Farm* is a gracious bed and breakfast in a large mid–nineteenth-century brick home set in seventy-five acres of riverside meadow. Rooms are bright and large with either queen-size or double beds and are reached from a broad central hallway and an elegant double staircase. Breakfast, served in a formal dining room, features fresh fruit and homemade muffins or scones in addition to the main dish. The setting is so quiet and lovely that it's tempting to forget sightseeing entirely and enjoy the walking or cross-country ski trails along the river, the gardens, badminton and lawn games, or the hammock on the wide porch shaded by the mulberry tree full of birds. Write Highland Farm, 148 County Farm Road, Dover 03820 or call (603) 743–3399.

The Ponds

Rides in fine restored carriages, sleighs, and wagons at *Point of View Farm* are more than transportation; they are, as owner Tyke Frost puts it, an "attempt to recapture some of the elegance that was part of the nineteenth century." Carriage rides are $15.00 per person (ages 12 and under $10.00). For a romantic evening Sue Frost prepares a full-course dinner after the carriage ride (with the coachman in top hat and tails) and serves it on antique china in a private Victorian dining room. Brunch combined with a surrey ride is $50.00 per couple. The Gathering Room is designed for birthday parties and other groups to have cake and ice cream after a hay or sleigh ride. Individual weekend rates are $5.00, $3.50 for children, and group rates start at $35.00 for a wagon or sleigh that holds fifteen or more people. Open year-round, reservations are required for special programs and are appreciated for individual and family visits. The farm is at 160 South Road, Deerfield 03074; telephone (603) 463–7974.

At *Harlow's Bread and Cracker Company,* in Epping, you can sample and buy scrumptious, not-so-traditional crackers; pizza, spicy cheddar, cracked pepper and ugly (blue cheese–based) to name just a few. Harlow's breads are equally delicious, and you can assemble a fine picnic with a creamy quiche, a delectable calzone, or a delicate focaccia. Don't leave without one of their delicious fig Newton bars, made from the Kennedy Bakery's original recipe. These are like nothing that ever came out of a box. This unusual bakery is on Route 27 within sight of Route 125. Write for their brochure (with mouth-watering descriptions of their crackers, which they ship), to 8 Exeter Road, Epping 03042, or call (603) 679-8883.

With the picnic basket freshly stocked from Harlow's, your next stop should be Pawtuckaway State Park. Along with its picnic area, this large park has both boat and canoe launch areas on the lake, two campgrounds with tent sites, a beach, and several hiking trails. One of these leads to the *Pawtuckaway Boulders,* a forest filled with huge glacial erratics that were broken from the cliffs on the two small mountains nearby and carried by the glacier to their present location a few thousand feet away in a valley to the east. The boulders vary in size, with some as long as 60 feet and over 30 feet high. Paths also lead to the summits of the three small mountains, two of which offer open views to the south. The campgrounds are open from late May to Columbus Day. Write Pawtuckaway State Park, RFD #1, Raymond 03077; call (603) 895–3301.

The *Sandown Depot Railroad Museum* is housed in a restored 1873 railroad station. It is thought to have been the busiest single-line railroad line in the country, with eighteen freight and sixteen passenger trains passing through Sandown each day. Most of the original railroad equipment is still in place, including the telegraph office. Open June through October, Saturday and Sunday, 1:00 to 5:00 P.M. Admission is free. The museum is on Route 121A in Sandown; call (603) 887–4621 for more information.

Inquire at the museum to see if the **Sandown Meeting House** is open to visitors. Built in 1773 and 1774, it is the finest and best-preserved church structure in the state. It still has its original hand-wrought hinges and latches on the paneled doors, as well as the square pews and slave gallery. (It surprises many to learn that owning slaves was a fairly common practice among wealthier New England families—although never to the extent it was in the South.) The pulpit is goblet-shaped, with a canopy that acts as a sounding board. If you are interested in early construction techniques, ask to see the loft, reached by a ladder from the gallery. Cross beams are staggered, and mortised joints are held by wooden keys. According to a local tale the church took longer to construct than was anticipated and the rum supply ran out. The workmen refused to continue until the supply was replenished.

Bed-and-breakfast accommodation is surprisingly rare in this part of the state, so visitors are happy to discover **Stillmeadow B&B,** one of several well-restored mid–nineteenth-century homes on Route 121 in Hampstead. Rooms are moderately priced, warm and welcoming, with private baths, nicely chosen color schemes, and pleasant views. Breakfast is served with elegance in the dining room and features home-baked breads and muffins. Write to P.O. Box 565, Hampstead 03841 or call (603) 329–8381.

Missing: A 48-Foot White Rock

*Y*ou will notice that we are fond of glacial erratics, those giant boulders the glaciers picked up in their travels and left off someplace else. But what promises to be one of the most striking of these seems to have disappeared. A book written in the 1930s refers to one in Raymond as follows: "South of the railroad station is an erratic boulder of white quartz that was transported several hundred feet. It is 48 feet long, 39 feet wide, and from 24 to 30 feet high. Two pine trees have found lodgement in crevices." We've looked for it, and everyone we've asked there is stumped. That's a pretty hefty rock to carry off, unless you're a glacier, so it must either be there (perhaps now covered in moss and pine needles) or have been a figment of someone's imagination. Many of these erratics were quarried (see Conway's), but quartz is an unlikely building stone. We've told you all we know. If you can find it and give us directions so we can include it in the next edition—or tell us when and how it disappeared—we'll send you an autographed copy.

PLACES TO STAY
ON THE SEACOAST
(*ALL AREA CODES* 603)

NEW CASTLE
Great Islander Bed and Breakfast, 62 Main Street, 03854-0135; 436–8536. Traditional bed and breakfast, 3 rooms, one with private bath. $75–$120, including continental breakfast.

PORTSMOUTH
The Inn at Christian Shore, 335 Maplewood Avenue, 03801; 431–6770. Bed and breakfast, six rooms, four with private bath. Double $65–$85 special weekends excepted, including full breakfast.

The Sise Inn, 40 Court Street, 03801; 433–1200. Elegant inn–bed and breakfast in an 1881 home, all private baths. Doubles $100 and up.

The Inn at Strawbery Banke, 314 Court Street, 03801; 436–7242 or (800) 428–3933. From Market Square, go two blocks east to Court Street, then north on Court Street. Bed and breakfast in a heritage home, seven rooms, all private bath, air conditioned. Doubles $75–$105 high-season, including full breakfast.

The Meadowbrook Inn, Interstate Highway Circle, 03801; 436–2700 or (800) 370–2727, FAX 433–2700. Exit 5 off I–95, motel style, 122 rooms, off-season double: budget $45, deluxe $55; high-season budget $90, deluxe $100.

SOUTH HAMPTON

The Inn at Kinney Hill, 96 Woodman Road, 03827; 394–0200. A converted private mansion on a hilltop, with three rooms and one suite. Double $95–$160.

HAMPTON BEACH

The Inn at Plaice Cove, 955 Ocean Boulevard, 03842; 926–1750. Motel style, 19 rooms. Double $85–$109, lower off-season.

HAMPTON

Lamie's Inn, 490 Lafayette Road, 03842; 926–0330. An inn in a 1740 home with a well-thought-of restaurant, 32 rooms. Double $75–$85.

DOVER

The Silver Street Inn, 103 Silver Street, 749–5673. In a former private mansion, replete with fine details—Austrian crystal doorknobs, imported stone fireplaces, hand-painted wall coverings—at moderate to high rates.

ROCHESTER

The Governor's Inn, 78 Wakefield Street, 03867; 332–0107. Suites in an elegant mansion in downtown Rochester; also a dining room with American cuisine.

DURHAM

The New England Center, 15 Strafford Avenue, 03824; 826–2815. A large (115 rooms), full-service hotel at the University of New Hampshire.

(For additional dining and lodging, remember that Portsmouth is only 12 miles away.)

PLACES TO EAT
ON THE SEACOAST
(ALL AREA CODES 603)

PORTSMOUTH
Karen's, 105 Daniel Street,
431–1948. Breakfast and lunch
daily, dinner Tuesday–Saturday.
Lunches $5.00–$6.00, dinner
$10–$15, most in low range.

Sakura, 40 Pleasant Street, off
Market Square, 431–2721. Lunch
Tuesday–Saturday, dinner
Tuesday–Sunday. Japanese. Sushi
combos $12–$48, other entrees
$8.00–$16.00, most around $14.

The Golden Egg, 960 Sagamore
Avenue, 436–0519. Simply
splendid breakfast and brunch
dishes, including omelets, French
toast, coffee cakes, quiches, and
muffins. It's open 7 days a week,
from 6:00 A.M. until 2:00 P.M.

DOVER
Alexander's, Portland Avenue,
742–2650. Traditional Italian
favorites with no surprises;
entrees are $6.00–$15.00

Newick's, 431 Dover Point Road,
exit 6W from the Spaulding
Turnpike west of the bridge;
742–3205. Open daily for lunch
and dinner, until 9:00 P.M.
Friday and Saturday. Seafood,
$6.00–$20.00, most around $10.

RYE
Hemingway's, 2000 Ocean
Boulevard, 964–1112. Daily,
lunch and dinner. Upscale
American. Entrees from $14.

HAMPTON
Lamie's Tavern, 490 Lafayette
Road, 926–0330. Chicken pot pie
to prime rib, in a colonial
setting. Entrees are
$9.00–$15.00.

HAMPTON FALLS
Luka's Greenhouse, 12 Lafayette
Road, 926–2107. Best known for
their Greek specialties, including
a bountiful sampler platter. Open
for lunch and dinner daily,
entrees $10–$17.

DURHAM
The Woods & Acorns at New
England Center, 15 Strafford
Avenue, 862–2815. Two dining
rooms, two menus, one stylish
and continental, one
Southwestern.

The Merrimack Valley

While the seaport provided the early links that built Portsmouth and Exeter, the size and force of the Merrimack River as it gathered waters from rivers and mountain streams in the north provided power for manufacturing that built the valley cities. Towns sprang up around the mills, and they continued to grow together. Manchester, the state's largest city, grew with the largest cotton-mill complex ever built. Even today, long after the mighty Amoskeag mills closed their doors, the remaining mill buildings continue to dominate the city's riverbank.

This swath up the center of the state is flatter than the land to the north or the west, and is characterized by rolling hills, small lakes, and a surprising amount of open space, especially north of Manchester.

The Merrimack Valley has never been tourist country. Most visitors pass through it on their way to the pleasures of the lakes and mountains farther north. Concord is occasionally visited for its historical sites, but Manchester's rich ethnic cultures are largely unnoticed.

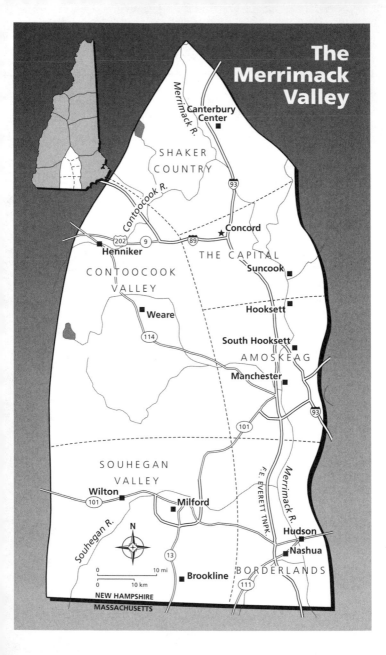

The
Merrimack
Valley

Merrimack R.

Canterbury
Center ■

SHAKER
COUNTRY

93

Contoocook R.

Concord ★

202
9
Henniker ■

THE CAPITAL

Suncook ■

CONTOOCOOK
VALLEY

Hooksett ■

Weare ■

114

South Hooksett ■

AMOSKEAG

Manchester ■

101

93

SOUHEGAN
VALLEY

Wilton ■
101

Milford
■

F.E. EVERETT TNPK.

Merrimack R.

Souhegan R.

N

Hudson ■

13

Nashua ■

0   10 mi
0   10 km

■ Brookline

BORDERLANDS

111

NEW HAMPSHIRE
MASSACHUSETTS

THE MERRIMACK VALLEY'S TOP PICKS

Nashua Historical Society
Abbot-Spaulding House
Mine Falls Park Heritage Trail
Ya Mama's
Robert Frost Homestead
Taylor Up and Down Sawmill
Derry Fire Department Museum
Upper Village National Historic District (Derry)
Chester Village Cemetery
Lawrence L. Lee Scouting Museum
Manchester Historical Association
Currier Gallery of Art
Amoskeag Fishway
Public archery ranges
Museum of New Hampshire History
Kimball-Jenkins Estate
Silk Farm Wildlife Sanctuary
St. Paul's School
Conservation Center (SPNHF)
Shaker Village
Tilton Arch
Fragrance Shop
St. Andrew's Episcopal Church
Pat's Peak
Beaver Brook Farm and Transportation Museum
Frye's Measure Mill
Birchwood Inn
Barrett House
Estelle M. Glavey Antiques

Borderlands

Although it is the state's second largest city, Nashua is as rarely explored as the back roads that surround it. An early manufacturing city, it retains much of its millyard area and the canal that provided the 36-foot vertical drop needed to run the machinery. This history, as well as life in Nashua during the industrial era, is well illustrated in the museum of the *Nashua Historical Society*. Changing exhibits feature subjects ranging from the role of Nashua in wars since the Civil War (arranged with interpretive and background information, as well as artifacts) to the interior of a local dry goods store. Children will enjoy the schoolroom and the player piano. Open year-round, Tuesday, Wednesday, Thursday, and Saturday afternoons. The museum is at 5 Abbott Street, just off Route 101A (Amherst Street), Nashua 03063; telephone (603) 883–0015.

Next door, and also owned by the Historical Society, is the elegant *Abbot-Spaulding House,* a Federal-style home built by the "Father of Nashua," Daniel Abbot. Both Daniel Webster and Franklin Pierce were frequent guests here; the furnishings were collected by the later owners and include several originals by designer Dexter Spaulding, as well as the family's collection of Sandwich glass. Although the Spauldings added some decorative details that were not there when the Abbots owned it, these are historically correct to the period and style of a leading family of the time. Open the same days as the museum next door.

For a view of Nashua's canal, walk along the *Mine Falls Park Heritage Trail.* The path borders the river and canal, forming a loop that can be reached from Riverside Street, where there is ample parking. A put-in on Mill Pond gives canoes and small boats access to the canal. You also reach the trail from the Millyard in downtown Nashua. For a trail map, contact the Nashua Conservation Commission at City Hall, 229 Main Street, Nashua 03061.

We'll use any excuse to go to Nashua just to have a chance to eat at **Ya Mama's,** a tiny piece of Italy hiding behind a Canal Street storefront. Having eaten our way through their entire menu, we've never hit a bad night or a dish that disappointed. The peppers Palermo, a bright plateful of roasted red peppers with garlic and provolone, or the lumache agliolio (snails served without their shells) are good beginnings, as is the zuppa di pesche, a steaming bowl of seafood in a savory broth frequently offered in the winter. Ya Mama's is at 42 Canal Street, Nashua 03061. Telephone (603) 883–2264.

A bright new urban bistro, **Timothy Michael's**, is upscale and casual in its atmosphere but not casual about its food. Presentation is attractive, and the dishes are a nice blend of innovation and tradition. Good sandwiches at lunch; moderate prices. Open for lunch Tuesday–Friday and dinner Tuesday–Sunday, with a Sunday jazz buffet 10:00 A.M. to 2:00 P.M., and live jazz in the Wine Bar Thursday–Sunday nights. 212 Main Street, Nashua; (603) 595–9334.

The **Robert Frost Homestead** on Route 28 was the home of the poet for the first decade of this century. Frost credited the years that he spent at this Derry farm with shaping his future by providing him with time and seclusion. The simple 1880s farmhouse, the barn, the brook, orchards, and stone walls mentioned in his poems are all here, much as they were during his time. A nature trail labeled with lines of his poetry winds through meadow and forest. Open daily mid-June to Labor Day and weekends only Memorial Day to mid-June and Labor Day to Columbus Day. Telephone (603) 432–3091.

Although sawmills are not rare in New Hampshire, the **Taylor Up and Down Sawmill** is the only up-and-down mill still operating. It is water-powered, with gears made of wood. The mill runs on Saturdays in July and August and four other days; ask for dates if you are interested in seeing it. Write Ballard State Forest, Island Pond Road, Derry 03038 or call (603) 271–3457.

On the first floor of the old fire station on Main Street is the **Derry Fire Department Museum,** with old photos, vintage lifesaving and firefighting equipment, and an old industrial pumper from a local mill. Look for the poem Robert Frost wrote for the Derry Fire Department after he lost control of a grass fire on his farm. Upstairs, collections of the **Derry Historical Society** cover

Robert Frost Homestead

subjects ranging from the local witch hazel, shoe, and egg industries to native son and astronaut Allan Shepard. Robert Frost is, of course, featured here. The museum is open either Saturday or Sunday on summer weekends, and by prior arrangement at other times. Call (603) 432–3188 for information.

The village of East Derry, a short detour on the way to the Taylor Sawmill, was the original settlement in 1719; today several fine old buildings, including the Village Hall, comprise the *Upper Village National Historic District.* A catalog of the buildings is available at the library, across from the Village Hall. A marker notes that the first white Irish potato in America was planted in the adjacent "Common Field."

North of Derry, the *Chester Village Cemetery* dates from 1751 and contains monuments by a number of colonial master stonecarvers. Look especially at the faces of the angels, a common motif on tombstones of the period. The story is that stoneworker Abel Webster, who lived in Chester in the 1700s, had a running theological quarrel with the townspeople, and to get even with them he put frowns on the faces of all the angels on the tombstones. At the crossroads of Routes 121 and 102 in Chester.

Amoskeag

Scouts and leaders will want to stop on the way into Manchester at one of the finest collections of Boy Scout memorabilia and books in the United States. The *Lawrence L. Lee Scouting Museum* is located at the headquarters of the Daniel Webster Council, where there are also picnic tables and camping facilities. Covering more than 3,000 feet of floor space, the museum houses more than 95 percent of all Scout books written in the United States, as well as historic uniforms, worldwide postage stamps commemorating scouting, and the original paintings used for covers of *Boy's Life*. Open 10:00 A.M. to 4:00 P.M. daily in July and August, weekends only in September through June, on Bodwell Road in Manchester; call (603) 669–8919 for more information.

Although it's hard to miss the red brick factory buildings that run the length of Manchester, you should visit the *Manchester Historical Association* for a closer look at how these mills shaped the past and present of this manufacturing city. On the main floor of the museum is an area for changing exhibits, which focus on a particular aspect of life or a period of history. These high-quality special exhibits give the curatorial staff a chance to look more closely at the subject and interpret the museum's many artifacts and documents. The museum encourages visitors to value their own collections, mementos, and family stories. Along with more recent history, the museum has a display of the earliest Indian relics found in New Hampshire, dating from the paleolithic era. The museum will tell you a lot about this hard-working city's blue-collar, down-to-earth history. There is a tiny gift shop on the first floor. The museum is free and nobody bothers you as you browse about, but your contribution will be appreciated even if there is no one to see you put it in the box. Open Tuesday through Friday 9:00 A.M. to 4:00 P.M. and Saturday, 10:00 A.M. to 4:00 P.M. You'll find it at 129 Amherst Street, Manchester; call (603) 622–7531.

Although you can wander on your own along the "mile of mills" and the adjacent blocks of brick company housing, you'll learn more if you join a walking tour led by Aurore Eaton, of *Local History Tours & Talks*. Aurore knows a lot about the history and architecture of the mills and Manchester, and her tours include a wealth of lively detail; call her to reserve a place at (603) 625–4827.

For a no-frills meal, walk a couple of blocks to the **Red Arrow Lunch.** It will be open, whatever the time of day; it has been since 1903. The menu includes stuffed cabbage, chicken pot pie, liver and onions, and meat loaf—you get the idea. Most entrees are priced under $5.00. Breakfasts are as generous as dinner and just as inexpensive. Open twenty-four hours, seven days a week, all year, at 61 Lowell Street (between Chestnut and Elm streets) in Manchester (603–624–2221).

An intimate atmosphere and a smashing menu combine to make **Richard's Bistro** our favorite place for dinner in Manchester. Individual overhead table lights and soft colors set the stage, but Richard's unique blending of flavors is the main act. He has a way with seafood—his creamy shellfish "chowder" is good enough to be dessert. The somewhat hurried lunchtime bustle gives way to a leisurely evening setting where you'll want to linger over one of his creative desserts. Open for lunch and dinner Monday–Saturday; moderate prices. It's at 36 Lowell Street; (603) 644–1180.

Manchester has a lot of little places to eat, many of them ethnic restaurants run by people who came from the country whose cuisine is featured. **The Athens,** on Central Street (603–623–9317), is good for hearty portions of Greek food, and a fine addition to the state's expanding Asian repertoire is **Hyung Jea,** on the corner of Chestnut and Manchester streets. Authentic Korean dishes are served in pleasantly simple surroundings. The menu describes the contents if patrons need help unraveling the mysteries of unfamiliar names. The Daeji Bul Go Ki, spiced grilled pork with crisp-cooked onions, is a good choice for those who like moderately spicy foods. Close to the Palace Theater, Hyung Jea is a convenient spot for an early dinner before a performance. They do not take credit cards and they are closed on Sunday; (603) 622–9377.

The French-Canadian influence is still strong in Manchester, with a daily French-language newspaper and the Association Canado-Americaine at 52 Concord Street (603–625–8577), whose library of more than 4,000 volumes centers on the development of French culture in North America. The west side of town, across the river, was the French-Canadian neighborhood, dominated by the impressive **Sainte Marie's Church.** The architecture is distinctive, and the stone interior is reminiscent of the cathedrals of Quebec and Montreal.

The **Currier Gallery of Art** displays permanent collections of American and European fine and decorative arts, as well as changing special exhibits and programs. Tours of the **Zimmerman House,** designed by Frank Lloyd Wright, begin here. The museum is open daily, except Tuesday, 11:00 A.M. to 5:00 P.M. and remains open until 9:00 P.M. on Friday. Admission is free Fridays from 1:00 until 9:00 P.M. The gallery is located at 192 Orange Street; telephone (603) 669–6144 for more information.

Behind the Manchester Historical Association, on Hanover Street between Chestnut and Pine streets, is a nicely designed and executed **wall mural** depicting the mill heritage that built Manchester. Continue up Hanover Street, away from the center of the city, to see some excellent examples of Victorian architecture lining both sides of the street.

The Merrimack River, whose power once operated machinery of the Amoskeag Mills, now produces electricity at the Amoskeag Hydro Station. When salmon were restored to the river a "fish ladder" was built to permit the fish to return to their spawning grounds. The Merrimack River Basin can support an adult salmon population of about 3,000, and visitors to the **Amoskeag Fishway** can watch the fish make their way up a series of stepped pools in late May. Large viewing windows allow visitors to observe fish at eye level. The fishway is open from late April until June with displays, programs, and films that illuminate the history, ecology, and wildlife of the river and of Manchester. Admission is free and the area is handicapped accessible. Enter from Fletcher Street, behind the TraveLodge at the Amoskeag Bridge; for exact opening times contact Public Service Company of New Hampshire, P.O. Box 330, Manchester 03105 or call them at (603) 626–FISH.

While hotels are plentiful in the city, B&B accommodation is rare. Travelers who prefer the surroundings of a finely kept home should call **Derryfield Bed & Breakfast.** Located in a quiet residential neighborhood with quick access to Interstate 93, Derryfield has surprisingly low rates. Breakfast is served overlooking the pool and surrounding woods, on a table set with fine china and crystal. Rooms must be reserved in advance at this small and very personal hostelry. The owner will meet guests at the airport, an unusual and welcome service. The B&B is at 1081 Bridge Street Extension, Manchester 03104; telephone (603) 627–2082 for reservations.

The only *public archery ranges* in New Hampshire are at Bear Brook State Park, northeast of Manchester. Maintained by the Fish and Game Department, each consists of fifteen targets. An additional four-target practice range is wheelchair accessible. The park includes several ponds, two marshes, and a wildlife refuge and offers swimming, tent camping, and fishing as well. Hiking trails, many of which become cross-country trails in the winter, cover the area.

One of the very few *Civilian Conservation Corps (CCC) camps* left in the northeast is in Bear Brook Park.

The buildings house a CCC Museum, a Snowmobile Museum, a Nature Center, and the Museum of Family Camping. All are open daily Memorial Day through Labor Day, and some weekends during spring and fall. Much of the park land itself was part of the CCC camp during the 1930s, and many of the picnic sites, hiking trails, recreation buildings, and roads you will enjoy on New Hampshire's public lands were built by the CCC. Write Bear Brook State Park, Allenstown 03275 or call (603) 485–9874.

The *Fitts Museum*, in nearby Candia, is a two-story house with a low hipped roof, two rooms of which are the original 1820 dwelling, with later Federal additions. Along with its antiques-filled rooms, it has a special event each Saturday afternoon in the summer—the only time it's open. Children's Day, herbs, spinning and weaving, or classic cars may be the subject, but you're bound to find activity at this free community museum. Open July and August on Saturdays, 1:00–4:00 P.M. Fitts Museum, Route 27, Candia.

The Capital

Although it is important as the center of government for the state, Concord is not a large city. (Incidentally, if you want to immediately label yourself as an outlander, pronounce Concord as you would the usual noun. In New England, it's pronounced "conquered.") Its manufacturing remained small, and it retains even now the appearance of a stately turn-of-the-century city, with its brick business blocks and government buildings of gray granite.

Blending into these buildings that surround the statehouse is the *New Hampshire Historical Society.* The sculpture above the columned granite façade is the work of Daniel Chester French, creator of the *Minuteman* statue in Concord, Massachusetts, and the seated Lincoln in Washington, D.C. The collections of the society on display include outstanding examples of New Hampshire furniture.

Most of the society's collections, however, have a new home nearby—walk to the farthest corner of the State House and look for the unusual iron gate on the opposite side of Main street. Newly created in a restored downtown building, the *Museum of New Hampshire History* brings the state's past alive in interactive exhibits that dramatize the first years of settlement and the state's growth right into modern times. Space for special exhibits is often brilliantly used to spotlight an era or a facet of New Hampshire's story.

A focal point is an original *Concord Coach.* Splendid in decorative detail, these coaches were as strong and as well constructed as they were beautiful. They were, in fact, so perfect in their design that from the 1820s to the early 1900s, during which time more than 3,000 of them were built in Concord, almost no changes were made in their construction. It was the most perfect traveling vehicle known to its times. Wells, Fargo and Company used them, and they have often been called "the coach that won the West."

The small museum shop in the historical society is an excellent source of publications on New Hampshire and its history. Many of these are privately printed and hard to find elsewhere.

With the new museum comes an admission charge of $5.00 for adults and $2.50 for ages six to eighteen; it's free on Thursdays from 5:00–8:30 P.M., the only day it has evening hours. It's open only in the afternoon on Sunday. Just off I–93 at exit 14, Eagle Square, Concord, (603) 226–3189.

Just north of Concord's downtown area, the **Kimball-Jenkins Estate** is the epitome of Victorian style and architecture. Eleven-foot ceilings, hand-carved oak woodwork, and the air of a well-run turn-of-the-century household characterize this home, which stands today exactly as it looked when it was the home of the Kimball family. The grounds that surround it are landscaped in period gardens. Visitors are taken on tours from June 1 until October 31, Tuesday through Sunday, 11:00 A.M. to 4:00 P.M. While appointments are not required, they are appreciated. The Kimball-Jenkins Estate is at 266 North Main Street in Concord; call (603) 225–3932.

Concord's arts calendar is enriched by the **Concord Community Music School,** which brings recitals, lunch-hour concerts, children's programs, and a variety of other classical and jazz performances to the area. For a complete schedule, write to the school at 23 Wall Street, Concord 03301 or call (603) 226–3151.

At the north end of Concord is the **Silk Farm Wildlife Sanctuary** and the headquarters of the New Hampshire Audubon Society. Trails traverse the forests and wetlands along the edge of Great Turkey Pond and cross orchards, hedgerows, and fields where visitors can see rare wildflowers as well as birds and small animals. Audubon House provides a year-round bird blind, an

If It Ain't Broke Don't Fix It

*B*uilt of New Hampshire granite (Is there any other kind?),
the State House in Concord is the oldest state capitol building
in the nation where the legislature still meets in its original
chamber.

excellent wildlife library, and a shop featuring a variety
of nature guides and gifts with a wildlife theme. It is
open Monday through Saturday, 9:00 A.M. to 5:00 P.M.,
and Sunday, 1:00 to 5:00 P.M. The library is open
Thursday and Saturday, 10:00 A.M. to 4:00 P.M. The New
Hampshire Audubon Society is at 3 Silk Farm Road (off
Clinton Street) in Concord, easily reached from Exit 2 off
Interstate 89. Call (603) 224–9909 for more information.

Silk Farm Road leads into the back entrance of **St. Paul's
School,** whose chapel has a finely executed fresco in the
oratory to the left of its entrance, a replica of Lorenzetti's
great fresco at Assisi. Two mobiles by Alexander Calder
are also on the campus; one is suspended from the
ceiling in the lobby of Memorial Hall, and the other is on
the grounds nearby. The outdoor mobile is stored from
November through March to protect it from the harsh
winter weather.

A small, but very attractive, bed and breakfast nearby
offers moderately priced rooms with private bath.
Breakfasts are served overlooking the well-tended
grounds of an avid gardener. Within a short walk,
between School and Franklin streets, is a neighborhood
filled with fine **Victorian houses,** many of which are
carefully restored. The bed and breakfast is not in a

restored historic home, but its comfort and hospitality are timeless. Write Charles and Harriet Ward, 43 North Fruit Street, Concord 03301 or call (603) 224–2620.

Across the river to the east, in Concord Heights, the Society for the Protection of New Hampshire Forests' **Conservation Center** maintains several buildings powered by alternative energy sources, as well as nature trails. This organization is responsible for the preservation of huge tracts of land throughout the state by either outright ownership, purchase of development rights, or helping private and governmental bodies in their efforts to save important lands and forests. You can tour their passive-solar building Monday through Friday, 9:00 A.M. to 5:00 P.M., free of charge. There is also a gift shop featuring environmental gifts and publications. Take East Side Drive (Route 132) north from Bridge Street (Route 9) to a left turn onto Portsmouth Street (you will pass the other end of this street going to the right shortly before the turn you want). The address is 54 Portsmouth Street (603–224–9945).

The Merrimack River Watershed Council sponsors free *Canoe Trips* on rivers in all parts of the state; you can bring your own canoe or rent one. For a schedule of trips, write to them at 54 Portsmouth Street, Concord 03301.

Shaker Country

ast Side Drive becomes Mountain Road, still Route 132, which leads to Canterbury and the beautifully maintained **Shaker Village.** Set on a hill among rolling meadows, this was once a thriving 4,000-

acre farm where 300 Shakers lived and worshiped in an atmosphere of common ownership, celibacy, and a strong work ethic. In the twenty-two buildings of the village you will see original examples of Shaker crafts in the furnishings of the houses. Skilled craftspeople are at work with wood, fiber, and plants creating baskets, boxes, brooms, and herbal crafts. Authentic lunches and dinners are re-created in the Creamery, where they use herbs from the village's garden. Guided tours begin on the hour and take about ninety minutes. A gift shop features Shaker reproductions and New Hampshire crafts. Thomas Merton once observed, "The peculiar grace of a Shaker chair is due to the fact that it was built by someone capable of believing that an angel might come and sit on it." Both that grace and its spiritual origins are evident throughout the village. Open May through December, 10:00 A.M. to 5:00 P.M., weekends April, November, and December. Admission is $8.00 for adults and $4.00 for children ages six to sixteen. Write Canterbury Shaker Village, 288 Shaker Road, Canterbury 03224 or call (603) 783–9511.

The town of Tilton is inextricably linked with the Tilton family, who were the generous benefactors of much of the town's artistic heritage. Charles Tilton, like many cultured men of his times, believed in the importance of public statuary and began to set about ornamenting his home town. Overlooking the town from a steep hillside on the opposite side of the river is the *Tilton Arch,* an exact replica of the Arch of Titus in Rome. Built of Concord granite, it rises 55 feet from its base, upon which lies a red granite lion. It is actually in the town of Northfield, and you can get there via the bridge at the monument on Main Street, turning left on the far side,

Tilton Arch

and going uphill to the Northfield Town Hall. Beside it, a dirt road leads to the top of the hill and the monument.

Five of Charles Tilton's statues remain. A marble allegorical statue of America—depicted as an Indian princess—stands on Main Street, as do statues symbolizing Europe and Asia. A zinc statue of Chief Squamtum now stands in a parking lot. An iron footbridge connects the town with an island, once the site of the Tilton summer house and now a shaded park.

Fine mansions still grace Tilton, and one of them, on West Main Street, is of particular interest. *The Black Swan* bed and breakfast is a beautiful preserved Victorian, filled with period architectural and decorative detail. One guest room includes a huge semicircular sitting room alcove with stained-glass panels over each of its seven windows. Each room has some distinctive antique feature or furnishing, and the dining room is fully paneled in oak with built-in china cupboards and a fireplace. The gardens and lawns sweep down to the riverbanks, overhung by shade trees. It's a thoroughly enjoyable resting place at moderate prices. Write The Black Swan at 308 West Main Street, Tilton 03276; call (603) 286–4524.

A number of fine craftspeople have studios in or near Tilton. The *Country Braid House* is both workshop and showroom for hand-braided wool rugs. Visitors are

Anybody Seen a Boulder Around Here?

*W*e were in Salisbury one Sunday afternoon with friends, searching for the Salisbury Boulder, of which we had a description and vague directions written in the 1930s, when roads were a bit different. We went over one of these nearly abandoned routes, climbing Oak Hill on little more than a track edging around the washouts and expecting the road to end at any point. When we finally came out onto a paved road—much to the surprise of the man who lived in the farmhouse at the corner—we asked him if he knew where we'd find the Salisbury Boulder. His eyes swept his rock-strewn pasture, where at least a dozen rocks were as tall as we were, and he repeated, "THE Salisbury Boulder?"

welcome to tour the workshop and learn about rug braiding. Those who would like to try their hand at it will find rug braiding kits for sale. Open Monday through Saturday, 9:00 A.M. to 4:00 P.M., on Clark Road in Tilton 03276 (603–286–4511).

Contoocook Valley

West of Concord lies an area of rolling farmlands and attractive villages. Hopkinton's wide Main Street is lined with trees and a number of homes of the colonial era. In the center of town on Main Street, the *New Hampshire Antiquarian Society* features a museum of early items. Open Monday, 1:00 to 5:00 P.M. and 6:30 to 8:30 P.M., and Wednesday, 9:00 to 11:00 A.M. and 1:00 to 5:00 P.M. Telephone (603–746–3825).

To see herbs and perennial flowers in an impressive garden setting, visit the *Fragrance Shop,* where you'll find 253 varieties of field-grown plants for sale. A walk in their gardens is pure joy, and the eighteenth-century barn is filled with wreaths, herb crafts, dried flowers, potpourri, and culinary herb blends as well as garden accessories, such as sundials and bee skeps. Open mid-April through December, Tuesday through Saturday, 10:00 A.M. to 5:00 P.M., on College Hill Road in Hopkinton (603–746–4431).

St. Andrew's Episcopal Church, in the village center, has particularly fine stained glass windows and, unlike most churches, has a thorough printed history of them, researched and written by retired St. Paul's teacher, John Archer. The latest of these windows to be added is by

Tiffany, a cross-and-lilies design much simpler than most Tiffany windows. You can get a copy of Archer's book and a key to the church from the office on weekdays.

The only Henniker on earth was named for a London merchant who was a friend of Royal Governor Benning Wentworth. New England College is in the center of town and gives it a lively air and a series of cross-country ski trails named for Marx Brothers movies. The toughest, which goes over a small mountain, is called "You Bet Your Life."

Skiing is not a new pastime in Henniker. For more than thirty years, the Patnaude family has operated one of New Hampshire's southernmost ski areas, *Pats Peak.* The mountain doesn't have the altitude of the White Mountains ski areas, but it has nineteen trails that are well groomed and well divided among the different skill levels; 90 percent snowmaking coverage extends the season. The food in the base lodge is homemade, and it's the kind of family ski area where you don't mind your kids skiing alone. Ski school, nursery, rentals, and other facilities are offered, and ticket sales are limited to the number of people that the lifts can comfortably handle without overcrowding. Write Pats Peak, Route 114, Henniker 03242 or call (603) 428–3245 or (800) 742–7287.

Fine dining and lodging are only a bit out of town at the *Colby Hill Inn,* a rambling New England hostelry that has been updated and renovated without losing its country inn flavor. The sixteen guest rooms, each with a private bath, and two with working fireplaces, are decorated with antiques. Details of decor and hospitality are all here—elegant bed linens, a full cookie jar, plenty of public rooms, and spontaneous and

Is it the Ghost of Ocean-Born Mary?

*O*n Gulf Road off Route 114 in Henniker stands a house
that was home to "Ocean-Born Mary." Shortly after her birth
on the high seas in 1710, the ship was attacked by pirates, but
their leader, on seeing the infant, promised to leave the ship
unharmed if the mother would name the child Mary, after his
mother. The pirate left a bolt of silk for Mary's wedding dress.
Mary lived to a ripe old age in her Henniker house. After her
death and until fairly recently, owners and neighbors have
reported seeing a black carriage drive up to the house at night
and stop, while a veiled figure descended and walked (or
floated) to the well, where it appeared to drop in a parcel before
leaving in the ghostly carriage. You can find Mary's tombstone,
labeled "Widow Mary Wallace," in the Quaker Cemetery on
Quaker Meeting House Road.

gregarious hosts. The location is perfect, surrounded by
meadows and a backyard where you can watch
pheasants as you sit in the perennial garden. In the
winter, part of the backyard becomes a skating rink for
guests. This is a full-service inn, so its prices are higher
than those of a typical bed and breakfast, beginning at
$85.00 for a double, including a full country breakfast.

The dining room at Colby Hill Inn serves dinner to the
public as well as to inn guests—and a fine dinner, too,
with a frequently changing menu. Chicken breast
stuffed with lobster is their signature dish. The salmon
is cooked to perfection. Dinner prices are in the upper-
moderate range, with most entrees $15.00 to $20.00.
The dining room is open year-round, Wednesday
through Saturday. Write Colby Hill Inn, The Oaks,
Henniker 03242 or call (603) 428–3281.

The entire Contoocook valley abounds with antiques shops, and the ***Fiber Studio*** features hand-dyed yarns, beads, and supplies for spinning, weaving, and knitting as well as hand-woven fabrics and sheep-related gifts. It's at 9 Foster Hill Road off Routes 202 and 9 in Henniker (603–428–7830).

The Souhegan Valley

Zahn's Alpine Guest House, on Route 13, will bring back immediate fond memories to anyone who has traveled in Bavaria, Austria, or Switzerland. It looks and feels exactly like those warm, hospitable mountain chalets that welcome travelers throughout the Alps. A big tile stove fills one corner of the Stube, which doubles as breakfast room and guest lounge. The pine post-and-beam construction with deeply overhung roof provides each of the guest rooms with a sheltered balcony—rimmed with window boxes of bright flowers in the summer. Alpine antiques, multicolored rag rugs, big feather pillows, and wrought iron fixtures complete the scene, but Zahn's has not fallen prey to the temptation to make it "Ye olde Alpine cute." It's the real thing, as is the hospitality; rates are below our moderate range. In the winter, kids can go for dogsled rides at the adjacent Christmas Tree Farm while parents cut their own tree. To reserve a room, write to Zahn's at P.O. Box 75, Milford 03055; call (603) 673–2334 or fax (603) 673–8415.

The owners of Zahn's have been asked so often for directions to area antiques shops that they've printed a little map for their guests showing twenty-two different shops.

A refreshing change from most small museums that are open only in the summer, **Beaver Brook Farm and Transportation Museum** in Mont Vernon, just north of Zahn's, is open Friday, Saturday, and Sunday, from Thanksgiving through New Year's Day, coinciding with the season of their adjacent Christmas Tree Farm. A narrow-gauge railroad, a fire engine display, a grist mill, Franklin Roosevelt's car, a Concord Coach, and a variety of sleighs, wagons, and buggies highlight the collections. Visits can be arranged at other times of year by advance reservation, but the museum is not open to casual drop-ins; there is no admission charge. Write to the museum at 78 Brook Road, Mont Vernon 03057, including your telephone number.

Water power was central to New Hampshire industry from the earliest days, and **Frye's Measure Mill** is still operated by an upright turbine driven by water from two ponds. Actively engaged in the making of fine round and oval wooden boxes, just as the first ones were made here in 1858, the mill also operates 1½-hour tours on Saturdays from June through October. The mill shop sells the boxes made here as well as other early crafts. Open April through December, from 10:00 A.M. to 5:00 P.M. The mill is on Davisville Road and Burton Highway in Wilton; call (603) 654–6581 for more information.

Not far from Frye's, on a winding country road that briefly becomes the main street of Wilton Center, **Stepping Stones Bed & Breakfast** stands among lovely tended terraced gardens. The gardens seem to move inside with you as you enter the sunny, plant-filled breakfast room, which overlooks the terrace through a solid wall of windows. Down comforters, wicker furniture, and vintage pieced coverlets make this lodging memorable, as does breakfast, which may feature corn quiche, almond omelet, or stuffed French toast as its main course. Pets and children are welcome here, but smoking is not. Stepping Stones, Bennington Battle Trail, Wilton Center 03086; telephone (603) 654–9048.

Six-tenths of a mile from Stepping Stones (follow the road toward Frye's, turning right and right again), you come to a stream. Park just before the bridge and follow the old road on foot to a pond, beyond which there is a lovely *cascade* on the left.

The rambling *Birchwood Inn* is as much a part of the town of Temple as the neighboring white-spired church. Its low-ceilinged dining room is decorated with murals believed to be by Rufus Porter, an itinerant nineteenth-century painter. This family-run inn changes its dining room menu nightly, with a choice of three entrees. Lamb is the house specialty, prepared in a variety of ways; one of the other two dishes is always seafood. On Route 45, a few miles off Route 101, in Temple, the inn is open year-round except April and serves dinner Tuesday through Saturday evenings from 6:00 until 9:00 P.M. (603–878–3285).

Along the border west of Nashua are the quiet country towns of Hollis, Brookline, and Mason, where roads wind among fields and through forests that sometimes meet overhead. *Silver Lake State Park* is here, with a good horseshoe-shaped shallow beach that is nearly empty on weekdays (but can get very crowded on summer weekends); admission is $2.50, with kids under eleven and seniors free. The adjacent, private **Wallace's Grove** also has a beach and a picnic grove in the pines. *Silver Lake Flea Market* is nearby, a huge area that on weekends is covered with dealers and locals cleaning their barns and attics. There's no predicting what you'll find there; call (603) 465–7677 for information and dates.

If you love herbs or perennial flowers, or just enjoy lovely gardens, follow the signs from Mason to **Pickety Place**. It's so far off the beaten path that you'll be sure you're lost long before you get there. Persevere and you will find, along with gardens, the cottage used by Elizabeth Orton Jones for Grandmother's House in her classic illustrations of *Little Red Riding Hood* and a shop brimming with handmade and herbal gifts. You can have an herbal luncheon in the cottage, which is open daily, but be sure to call for reservations, since a lot of people manage to find their way here. Pickety Place, Nutting Hill Road, Mason; (603) 878–1151. When you

The Early Bird Gets the Surprise

*I*t's not unusual for flea market dealers to arrive the night before and camp in trucks so they can set up early in the morning, but Gerald St. Louis probably won't do it again, at least not at Hollis Flea Market. He and two boys who were helping him were startled one night in 1977 by an 8-foot furry creature, which left footprints over 16 inches long. Mr. St. Louis didn't wait to measure the prints: he jumped in his truck and left with the boys. Two other dealers, unaware of St. Louis's experience, described having their truck shaken by big furry hands, and they left pretty quickly too. The tracks found by their truck matched the others.

But He Wasn't Born on the Fourth of July

Uncle Sam was born in a small farmhouse in Mason, on the road between Mason and Brookline. Sam Wilson supplied the army with barrels of beef and pork in the War of 1812, and each barrel was stamped "US" to distinguish it from barrels destined elsewhere. A dockhand on the Hudson River, where they were being loaded, was asked what the initials stood for and replied that they were Uncle Sam's meat, using the name everyone called Sam Wilson. Somehow it stuck as a symbol, and artists soon created the familiar caricature. There's a sign in front of the house.

leave Pickety Place, you can go on to New Ipswich instead of backtracking—or you can approach Pickety Place by following signs from Route 31 in Greenville.

The **Barrett House** in New Ipswich, one of the state's most outstanding Federal mansions, remained in the Barrett family from its construction in 1800 until it was given to the Society for the Preservation of New England Antiquities in 1948. Ornamented with pilasters and a central pediment, it is said to have been built as a wedding present to Charles Barrett, Jr., from his father. Furnished with the best that each generation of the family could afford, including imported china and even a glass harmonica, the house interprets the life of a wealthy New England textile manufacturer and farming family over the course of several generations. Teas with guest lecturers are held throughout the summer and special events such as a late May antiques show highlight their schedule. Open Thursday through Sunday, June 1 through October 15, with house tours hourly from 12 noon to 4:00 P.M. Admission is $4.00 with special rates for seniors and children. Take Route 124 to New Ipswich, then Route 123A. You can write them at Main Street, New Ipswich 03071, or telephone (603) 878–2517.

In the same town there is another house filled with antiques, but these are all for sale. ***Estelle M. Glavey Antiques*** fills an entire home, not with showrooms, but with fully furnished rooms of museum-quality antiques. This is no jumble of merchandise. Everything, from the oriental rug on the floor to the china on the table and the flame-stitched wing chair by the fire, is just as it would be in a home—but all for sale and clearly tagged with a price, not a code. The surprise is that the pieces are very reasonably priced, considering their quality and condition. Open all year daily except Monday on Route 124 (603–878–1200).

Windblown Ski Touring Center keeps 20 miles of trails well groomed for cross-country skiers. Along with their waxing shed and restaurant, the center offers a warming hut with "sleeping bag accommodations." The views are spectacular. It's on Route 124, 3 miles west of the town of New Ipswich; call (603) 878–2869 for more information.

PLACES TO STAY
IN THE MERRIMACK VALLEY
(ALL AREA CODES 603)

In Nashua–Manchester areas, most of the major chains have hotels, but for inns or bed-and-breakfast lodgings, you'll need to look a little farther north, or west.

BEDFORD
Bedford Village Inn, One Village Inn Lane (off Route 101), 472-2001. In a converted barn behind the farmhouse, stylish rooms with all the comforts, starting at $145.

LONDONDERRY
Breezy Hill Bed and Breakfast, 119 Adams Road, 03053; 432-0122. A nineteenth-century farmhouse near the Manchester airport. Moderate.

CONCORD
A Touch of Europe Bed and Breakfast, 85 Centre Street, 226-3771. In a neighborhood of fine Victorian homes, with a German-style breakfast.

Centennial Inn, 96 Pleasant Street, 225-7105 or (800) 267-0525. The newest and most elegant lodgings in the capital; Victorian, but light and warm.

The dining room serves all three meals, with vegetarian and heart-healthy options. Doubles are $125–215. Restaurant moderate.

Comfort Inn, 71 Hall Street, 06030; 224-9534 or (800) 221-2222. Not the ordinary chain hotel, this new hotel is stylish and immaculately maintained. Moderate rates.

LOUDEN
Lovejoy Farm B&B, 268 Lovejoy Road, 783-4007. In a 1700s Colonial close to the Shaker Village, the rooms all have private baths; hearty breakfasts.

The Wyman Farm Bed and Breakfast, 22 Wyman Road, 03301-1014; 783-4467. Three guest rooms with private baths and sitting areas, full breakfast (from a menu selected the night before) and afternoon tea tray, at $55 to $75.

HOPKINTON
Country Porch Bed and Breakfast, 281 Moran Road, 03229; 746-6391. Fine views from its wraparound porches and a hearty breakfast at moderate rates. Take Hatfield Road off Route 9 to the pavement's end and turn left to Moran Road.

HENNIKER
Don't plan to stay near Henniker on Mother's Day weekend; it's

graduation at the local college, and rooms are booked two years in advance.

Henniker House Bed and Breakfast, 2 Ramsdell Road, 03242; 428–3198 or (800) 809–5826. A Victorian house, with king and twin rooms at $60–$80. Full-course breakfasts in the solarium overlooking the river.

WEARE
Weare-House Bed and Breakfast, 76 Quaker Street, 529–2660. An early nineteenth-century farmhouse with barn and animals, off Route 114, with moderate rates.

TEMPLE
The Birchwood Inn, Route 45, 878–3285. Breakfast included, doubles $60–$70. See text for description of dining room.

PLACES TO EAT
IN THE MERRIMACK VALLEY
(ALL AREA CODES 603)

SALEM
Millstone Manor, 43 Pelham Street, 898–1918. Eclectic Italian; innovative dishes at $10–$20 for entrees. Excellent luncheon salads.

MANCHESTER
Cafe Pavone, 75 Arms Drive, 622–5488. A good use for a part of the old mill complex off Bridge Street, with a bright decor and mix-and-match pasta menu, as well as good seafood and meat entrees, all in the $7.00–$18.00 range.

BEDFORD
Bedford Village Inn, One Village Inn Lane (off Route 101), 472–2001. Choose between the old New England farmhouse dining rooms or the bright, airy sunporch; the menu puts a new spin on old favorites. A bit pricey, but very good.

Shorty's Mexican Road House, Route 101, 472–3656. Mexican plus, in an upbeat mood. When they say hot, they aren't wimps about it. Open every day for lunch and dinner, with entrees starting around $7.00.

CONCORD
Angelina's, 11 Depot Street; 228–3313. Pasta made fresh daily (you can watch) for this chic restaurant. Open for dinner every night. Veal is a specialty.

Caffenio, 84 North Main Street; 229–0020. Good for lunches and coffees, if you don't mind balancing them on the saucer-sized tables.

Capital City Diner, exit 13 off I-93; 228-DINE. Three meals daily at budget prices.

Hermano's Cocina Mexicana, 11 Hills Avenue (one block off main Street); 224-5669. A wide choice of beers—Mexican and otherwise—accompany traditional south-of-the-border dishes and some unusual ones. Lunch Monday–Saturday, dinner every night.

TILTON

Le Chalet Rouge, 321 West Main Street, 286-4035. A frequently changing menu of French classics, served Tuesday–Saturday evenings. Moderate-to-pricey; not all cards are accepted.

Tilt'n Diner, exit 20 off I-93, at the junction of US 3 and Route 140; 286-2204. A stainless steel classic, serving three meals daily at budget prices.

HENNIKER

Daniel's Restaurant and Pub, Main Street, 428-7621. Sandwiches, pastas, and light and full-sized entrees in a pub atmosphere overlooking the river. All sandwiches are $6.00, entrees $10–$17, light entrees (which include venison sausage) $7.00–$9.00.

Que Pasa Restaurant, Route 114, 428-TACO. Mexican food, as you probably guessed, at moderate prices.

Meetinghouse Inn and Restaurant, Flanders Road, 428-3228. Rooms with private bath; hot tub and sauna extra; well-regarded dining room at upper-moderate rates.

MILFORD

The Colonel Shepard House, 29 Mont Vernon Street, 672-2527. Ribs and pasta dishes, most $8.00–$16.00, burgers, sandwiches, and bar snacks in the adjoining taproom.

Elisha's Restaurant, 437 Nashua Street, 673-8764. Char-broiled meats, barbecue and seafood, $8.00 and up.

The Mile Away, 52 Federal Hill Road, 673-3904. Continental menu, $15–$19.

MASON

Parker's Maple Barn, Brookline Road, 878-2308. Maple sugar house with a rustic country restaurant that serves breakfast and lunch Monday–Wednesday, three meals other days.

The Monadnock Region

Word has it that Mount Monadnock is no longer the second most climbed mountain in the world. With motorized access to Fujiyama's summit, fewer people are climbing it, so Monadnock may now be number one. Whichever, its rocky ledge summit on a fine summer day is definitely not off the beaten path. But its broad-shouldered cone standing alone with no other mountains for company is the focal point for an entire region. Views of it provide the backdrop for towns miles away, from Jaffrey, where most of the mountain lies, to Keene. On clear days it can be seen from as far away as Boston and the Green Mountains of Vermont.

Geologically, the mountain is the definitive *monadnock*, a mass of rock more durable, hence more resistant to erosion and glacial action, than the land around it. It is this mountain for which the geological phenomenon was named. The rest of the land of this southwest corner of New Hampshire is rolling, accented with small mountains and lakes. Only one city, Keene, is located in the entire area. It, and Peterborough, provide the cultural and business centers, but the smaller towns are surprisingly active, with their own museums, concert

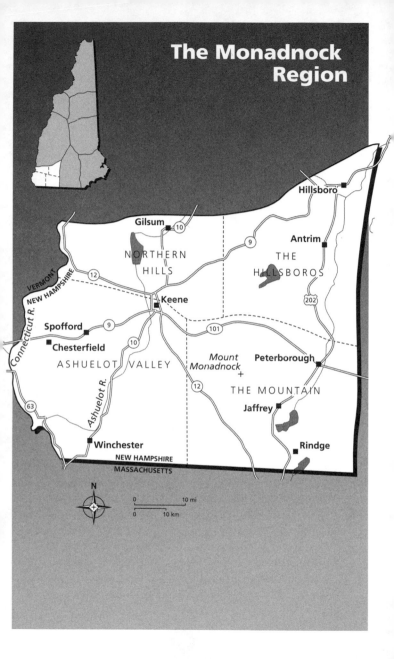

The Monadnock Region

Hillsboro

Gilsum ⑩

Antrim

⑨

NORTHERN HILLS

THE HILLSBOROS

VERMONT

NEW HAMPSHIRE

⑫

Keene

202

Connecticut R.

Spofford ⑨

⑩

101

Mount Monadnock +

Peterborough

Chesterfield

ASHUELOT VALLEY

THE MOUNTAIN

Ashuelot R.

⑫

Jaffrey

63

Rindge

Winchester

NEW HAMPSHIRE

MASSACHUSETTS

N

0   10 mi

0   10 km

THE MONADNOCK REGION'S TOP PICKS

Hillsborough Center
Fox State Forest
Greenfield State Park
Peterborough Historical Society Museum
New England Marionette Opera
Pack Monadnock Mountain
Cathedral of the Pines
Amos J. Blake House
Rhododendron State Park
Wyman Tavern
Barry Faulkner mural
Archive Center of the Historical Society of Cheshire County
Horatio Colony House Museum
Covered bridges
Swanzey Historical Museum
Stonewall Farm
Chesterfield Gorge
Park Hill
Old Academy Museum
Bascom's Maple Farms

series, and theater groups. The bandstands that decorate the commons of Monadnock's towns are not there just to take pictures of. Painters, writers, and musicians have found a haven in this area for a century, giving it a rich tradition in the arts.

The Hillsboroughs

Visitors from outside New England often comment on the apparent lack of originality displayed in the naming of towns here. In one area will be found town after town with the same name prefixed by the four points of the compass or by *Center, Upper,* or *Lower,* or suffixed by *Falls, Mills, Junction, Street,* or *Depot.* The reason has to do with the town system of government, which was often based upon the original land grants. Large parcels of land were settled with several villages springing up within the boundaries of a town. Hillsborough is a good example. Within the limits of the town are Hillsborough, Hillsborough Center, Hillsborough Upper Village, and Hillsborough Lower Village.

The commercial center of the town is called **Hillsborough** (and Falls Village and Mill Village) and lies along Route 9. **German John's** (603–464–5079), a bakery featuring fine European breads and pastries, is in the ground floor of an old commercial building at the intersection of Routes 9 and 149, at 1 Bridge Street. Their goodies are just right for a pick-me-up, and their soft pretzels are a local legend. Park on the main street since Bridge Street is steep and narrow.

The **Town Offices and Library** on School Street (603–464–3595) are in the former Governor John B. Smith Mansion, a composite Colonial Revival and Queen Anne–style building, that features exquisite woodwork and ornate gold arabesque ornamentation of its ceilings. It's open weekday business hours. Continuing on out School Street, you will eventually come to Hillsborough Center. The road itself is worth the drive, passing well-tended countryside, old homes and farms, and between some of the finest stone walls in the state.

Fox State Forest is a 1,448-acre area of managed forest that contains plantations of exotics (trees that do not grow here naturally) and some unusual protected natural areas as well. One of these is a black gum, or tupelo, swamp. This tree is common to the south but rarely found in New England. A ravine of mature hemlock and one of the state's rare stands of virgin forest are here, as well as a true sphagnum bog formed by a floating mat of moss filled with rare wild plants. More than 20 miles of hiking trails wind through the forest; cross-country skiers are welcome on the trails in the winter, but there are no other recreation facilities here, since this is a forest, not a park. You are welcome to picnic on the grounds (they have a few tables) as long as you respect the "carry-in, carry-out" policy. Open year-round from dawn to dusk. Look inside the mailbox by the entrance for a trail guide. Write Fox State Forest,

Hillsborough Center Road, P.O. Box 1175, Hillsborough 03244 or call (603) 464–3453 for more information.

Just past Fox State Forest, you'll find the **Inn at Maplewood Farm**, a big old 1794 colonial farmhouse with a welcoming columned porch. It has four newly renovated rooms, all with private bath, period furnishings, decorative antiques, and vintage radios. A three-course breakfast in the cheery dining room features homemade breads and dishes such as cream-basil-shirred eggs with maple glazed ham or an asparagus and goat cheese frittata with an almond and anise *pane del pescatore*. The family collection of antique radios is not just for decoration—the inn has its own in-house radio station that broadcasts 1920s–1940s radio programs to each room. The energetic hosts, the Simoes, are bursting with information on the area. Double-room rates of $75–$85 include breakfast. It's at 447 Center Road, P.O. Box 1478, Hillsborough 03244. Take School Street from the center of town, it turns into Center Road. Phone (603) 464–4242 or (800) 644–6695.

Big Mack Attack

A block downhill from the traffic light on Route 149 (Bridge Street) in Hillsborough, make a left turn onto River Street, just before the bridge, to find yourself in the state's most unusual open-air museum. There's no sign and no entrance gate, but you know you're there when you're suddenly surrounded by Mack trucks of every stripe. Delivery trucks, a vintage Texaco tank truck, and dozens of others line both sides of the street, as though you'd time-traveled back into the parking lot of a long gone roadside diner.

Hillsborough Center is among New Hampshire's loveliest towns, its houses set around a circular road on a slight slope, with two churches. The entire center of the village is webbed with stone walls, testament to the number of rocks that northern New Englanders have had to pull out of their farmlands over the centuries. A well-preserved town pound, built to keep stray animals out of neighbors' gardens, completes this almost perfect village scene. Just outside of town, rows of nearly perfect double-stone fences border the fields of two exceptionally beautiful hillside farms.

Near the Town Pound and the old schoolhouse, the father and son team of *Raymond and Jonathan Gibson* produce heritage quality, lead-free *pewter* in contemporary and traditional designs. Some of their work is in the Boston Museum of Fine Arts. In addition to plates, bowls, tankards, and chalices, they produce candlesticks and collector-quality spoons. To inquire about the repair of old pewter, write 18 East Washington Road, Hillsborough Center 03244; (603) 464–3410.

If you continue out East Washington Road, you will come to *Sage Knoll Herbs and Perennials*, a labor of love for Joan Phipps, who has collected a large variety of old herb and perennial varieties from cellar holes and roadsides, as well as tracking them down in heritage gardens. Her plant list has more than 165 perennials and herbs for sale. She doesn't ship, so you'll just have to visit with this fascinating horticulturist at 955 East Washington Road; (603) 478–5461.

In East Washington, follow the road around to the right along the shore of the millpond, left at the meetinghouse, and up the hill. On the right you will see the red house and barn of **Bifrost Farm**, a Morgan horse and shiitake mushroom farm. In addition to breeding fine horses, Lynn and Richard Cook grow over 500 pounds of fresh mushrooms every week, year-round. The best part is that you can buy some to take home. They welcome visitors, and you can see the carefully controlled rooms where the fungi are raised. They're at 2402 East Washington Road, East Washington 03280; (603) 495–3730.

A few miles farther up the same road, **Eccardt Farm** in East Washington is a real, operating dairy farm, where you can watch the milking, see an amazing collection of live birds including peacocks and exotic chickens and ducks, and see sheep, goats, and rabbits. In the spring, you can help them turn sap into syrup. Milking times are 3:30 and 7:00 P.M. They also have a fascinating collection of old farming equipment including tractors and tools. This is a multigenerational farm, a real place without glitz and a great experience for kids; (603) 495–3157.

Just west of Hillsborough on Route 9 is the boyhood **home of Franklin Pierce,** New Hampshire's only native son to become President of the United States. The mansion is a more elegant residence than was common in rural New Hampshire when it was built in 1804 and its interior has some surprises in store for those who think of New England decor as having been in somber puritan colors. The stenciling and decorative painting, which has been restored from remaining paint samples, is in vivid reds; the original Balfour mural wallpaper in the parlor is among the finest examples in any restored home. Hillsborough's active Historical Society, which maintains and staffs the house, also holds monthly programs, with speakers who explore some facet of New

Hampshire history. These are usually held at the Pierce Homestead on the fourth Monday of the month, at 7:00 P.M. You can call the house for a schedule. Open Memorial Day to Columbus Day, Saturdays 10:00 A.M. to 4:00 P.M., Sundays 1:00 to 4:00 P.M., and Fridays in July and August, 10:00 A.M. to 4:00 P.M. It's at the intersection of Routes 9 and 31; (603) 478–3165.

This was Pierce's boyhood home; to see the house where he took his new bride (not open to the public), turn left from the driveway and cross Route 9. Begin counting houses at the corner, and the Pierce house is the fourth on the right. Continue on down that road, passing a small cluster of homes with a little church at Union Village, where the pavement ends. Just beyond, on the unpaved road, you'll cross a fine pair of stone arches, which you can see best from the little road that goes off to the right just after you cross them. A brochure with a **_Self-Guided Walking Tour_** of the Franklin Pierce neighborhood is available at the Mansion. The walk is about a mile in length and the brochure describes the lives, times, and structures that surrounded the future President as he grew up.

Hillsborough has five of these fine **_stone arch bridges_**. One is bypassed by the new US 202 at its intersection with Route 9 just west of the town of Hillsborough. Another is at the intersection of Shedd Jones and Beard Roads. This one stands in the open, where you can get a good view of it from both directions. From the Pierce house, turn right, then right again down the hill onto Shedd Jones Road. Follow it until you come to the intersection with Beard Road, and you'll see the double-arched bridge right ahead of you. If you turn right,

Beard Road will take you back to Route 9, passing a riverside *swimming hole* maintained by the town, but without lifeguards.

If, however, you go left on Beard Road, you will cross another stone bridge, this one spanning *Gleason's Falls*, which you can best see by following the path downstream a few yards. The river continues to cascade from pool to pool through a jumble of moss-covered boulders for a little way below the falls; notice the long groove the water has carved in the ledge as it has created a channel. *Be careful* above the upper pools, since the pine-needle floor of the forest is very slippery and the drop a substantial one. If you continue on Beard Road a very short way and turn right onto Gleason Falls Road, you'll come out just above Hillsborough Center, on the road to East Washington. A left turn onto Gleason Falls Road does *not* take you back to Route 31 where you began, even though maps show it. Trust us on this one.

As you go west on Route 9, look for a double-stone arch bridge beside the road. It's worth a stop here to walk around to the upstream side for a better picture of what it looked like in the nineteenth century. You can go down under the present bridge to see the stonework of the old bridge as well as the river as it continues downstream through a mass of boulders.

Close to this bridge is the studio and shop of the noted glass artist, *Chris Baker-Salmon*. His work, which is sold in stylish decorator shops, is both elegant and usable; you really want to savor wine from one of his glasses with the colored-glass flower encased in its long graceful stem. Prices here are far below those in the shops he supplies, and seconds—those with minor flaws that only make them more interesting—are less than half regular studio prices. Stunning bowls are $25 and goblets $14–$15. Window medallions, which make good Christmas tree ornaments, are under $4.00. He's not open Saturdays in the summer, but someone's usually there; the studio is closed January through March.

In a grove of tall pines west of Hillsborough, **Pine Haven Cabins** is one of the few places to eat along the route, as well as a place to stay. Started in 1940, several of these homey, old-fashioned cabins have two bedrooms, and all have good mattresses and showers in the bathrooms. One has a kitchenette. These are rustic, modestly priced cabins where the smell of the pine woods is like perfume. In the memorabilia-filled dining room, breakfast is served all day, from 7:30 A.M. and lunch is served until 7:30 P.M. In addition to sandwiches, steaks, and burgers, they surprise you by offering Cornish Pastys for $3.95, natural ice cream, and homemade pies and cakes. It's at North Branch Road, Routes 9 and 31, Hillsborough 03244; (603) 588–6803.

Blues fans may have heard of **The Rynborn**, in the center of Antrim, just south of Route 9 on either Route 31 or US 202. Thursday through Sunday evenings, year-round, the Rynborn features big names in blues, with New England and nationally known groups and artists. The usual admission price is $5.00; (603) 588–5162.

The Mountain

The white-spired meeting house in **Hancock** is said to be the most-photographed church in the state, although it is hard to understand how such a statistic is determined. The entire town of Hancock invites photography with its neat rows of fine old buildings along the main street. *The Hancock Inn,* has been welcoming travelers for more than two hundred years. One of its guest rooms has wall murals painted by the itinerant artist Rufus Porter.

Greenfield State Park reserves one sandy beach just for campers who have settled into its spacious, wooded tent sites and has another one for day visitors and picnickers. This is one of the rare places where you can rent a boat either for the fishing or to enjoy the quiet of Otter Lake. One of the smaller of New Hampshire's state parks and one of the least known, it is a perfect retreat for nature lovers, swimmers, and those who seek a place to paddle their canoe in peace. Write the park at P.O. Box 203, Greenfield 03047 or call (603) 547–3497.

Historical societies perform several valuable services to their towns, such as storing and preserving records of long-closed schools and businesses, providing a safe home for old photographs, maps, and books that would otherwise be lost, and offering a clearinghouse for historical and genealogical information. A few maintain museums based on purchases or gifts of local artifacts, furnishings, and property.

The *Peterborough Historical Society Museum* is one of the finest historical museums of any society in the state. Along with exhibition rooms featuring early tools and antiques, they have in the several buildings of their complex a complete Victorian parlor, a replica of a country store, a colonial-era kitchen, and a restored mill house. Open year-round, Monday through Friday, 1:00 to 4:00 P.M. Tours available in July and August; cost furnished in period antiques. A kitchen, parlor, music room, and reconstructed schoolroom are part of the museum, as are displays of military and firefighting memorabilia. A small shop, filled with local crafts, New England food specialties, soaps, and gifts, uses original country-store counters, furnishings, and cash register. Admission is free. Open late May to mid-October, Saturday, 10:00 A.M. to 4:00 P.M., and Sunday, 1:00 to 4:00 P.M. Write the Blake House, On the Common (P.O. Box 87), Fitzwilliam 03447 or call (603) 585–6642.

One of the largest stands of wild rhododendron north of the Allegheny mountains is in Fitzwilliam at **Rhododendron State Park.** The fifteen acres of large shrubs bloom by mid-July in a riot of huge flower clusters against glossy, deep green leaves. At any time of year the trails through this park are bordered by masses of broad evergreen leaves and the thick tangle of trunks and branches that support them. An adjoining wildflower trail was created by the Fitzwilliam Garden Club. Native plants are labeled in the open woodland that borders the path. It is a lovely, quiet, and cool spot, with 1 mile of easy walking. Follow the signs off Route 119.

back road that branches off Route 12, not far north of e rock ledges, gives more views of Monadnock as well a stone bridge. It brings you to Route 124 and into rlborough. At the intersection with Route 101 is the mestead Bookshop. Strong in local history, they e several shelves of long-out-of-print books on New pshire as well as a travel section well stocked with works of explorers and adventurers. In addition to ng nearly 50,000 used books, you will meet the t people there. Their book search service ferrets

The Thirteenth Wife

*J*oseph Smith, founder and leader of the Church of the Latter-Day Saints, died suddenly in the 1840s, while Brigham Young was conducting a revival meeting in Peterborough. While still in Peterborough, Young was chosen to replace him as the Mormons' leader, and when he left for Utah, some time later, 136 "leading citizens" of the town followed him, including one young woman who became his thirteenth wife.

$1.00. The museum is at 19 Grove Street (P.O. Box 58), Peterborough 03458 (603–924–3235).

Peterborough has a theatrical heritage: Bette Davis began her career here at Mariarden, a theater summer school, in 1926, as a dancing fairy in *A Midsummer Night's Dream.* The town's newest theater is the **New England Marionette Opera,** which stages full productions of operas such as *La Bohème* and *Madame Butterfly* in a 135-seat theater designed especially for the 32-inch actors. So real and captivating is the performance that the little figures are called back for curtain calls and stopped by applause following arias. Technique is so flawless that even those who don't care for opera enjoy the performances. The theater is on Main Street, Peterborough 03458; for reservations call (603) 924–4333.

The **Sheiling Forest** provides pleasant walking through fields and forests, following stone walls built by farmers of long ago trying to clear their fields of the oversupply of granite boulders with which New Hampshire was blessed. These are easy, level walks. On Saturdays there are programs for small woodlot owners on the care and management of woodlands. Open daily dawn to dusk year-round on Old Street Road in Peterborough.

Peterborough residents evidently have a taste for good food, since there are a number of culinary havens in town. The **Kernel Bakery** was making flaky croissants for Monadnock-region breakfast tables long before *croissant* became a household word. And they are half the price of inferior products elsewhere. Their doughnuts, Danish, cookies, Eccles cakes, and breads are just as good. You can get a cup of coffee here to go with your breakfast pastry, but alas, not a cup of tea. Closed Sunday, Monday, and middays. You'll find the Kernel Bakery on Jaffrey Road (Route 202) in Peterborough; call (603) 924–7930.

Although not as well known as its sister mountain, **Pack Monadnock** in Miller State Park offers easy access to mountaintop views extending from Boston to the White Mountains and Vermont. A fee is charged for use of the auto road to the summit or you can climb it on foot by any of three hiking trails, each about 1½ miles long. Picnic areas and an observation tower are at the open summit. The entrance is on Route 101 opposite the Temple Mountain ski area.

Del Rossi's Trattoria does a good job with the unlikely combination of a real Italian restaurant and a first-rate country music venue. Neither is ever compromised for the other. Get their schedule and reserve early for big names, or go on a weeknight just for the food, which includes fettuccine with shiitake mushrooms (from Bifrost Farm, of course), peas, and Marsala or a breast of chicken stuffed with basil and fresh tomatoes in a Gorgonzola sauce. About twenty entree choices tempt

you, at $9.00–$14.00, a little more for shellfish. The wine list is also excellent. It's on Route 137, in Dublin, just north of Route 101; (603) 563–7195.

The Friendly Farm sits at the edge of the woods near Dublin Lake, where kids and adults can meet, pet, and get to know farm animals. Baby animals predominate and love to be fed. Open 10:00 A.M. to 5:00 P.M. daily from late April through Labor Day, and weekends until mid-October, weather permitting. Half a mile west of the lake, Main Street (Route 101), Dublin; (603) 563–8444.

Cathedral of the Pines is an outdoor church as well as a national memorial to those who lost their lives in wartime military service. Services are held here by people of all faiths, using the various altars and wood "chapels." The Memorial Tower holds a peal of Sheffi bells and a set of four Norman Rockwell bas-relief memory of the women who served in the military. when Cathedral of the Pines is not open for service can walk through the grounds, a forest of tall pine a hillside, with views of Monadnock, Kearsar southern Vermont. Off Routes 202 and 119 in call (603) 899–3300 for more information.

Where other towns may be "postcard towns," F is a "Christmas card town." Its white tow stately homes set around the snow-cover make it a favorite for artists and photograp greeting cards. One of these buildings on t the **Amos J. Blake House,** a museum mai Fitzwilliam Historical Society. Built in 18 home and law office of a well-respec leader. His law office is intact, and out books for customers in all parts of the country. Open Monday through Friday, 9:00 A.M. to 5:00 P.M., and Saturday and Sunday, 9:00 A.M. to 4:30 P.M. Call (603) 876–4213 for more information.

Ashuelot Valley

Keene's main street is lined for several blocks by beautifully cared-for private residences covering all architectural periods since the mid-eighteenth century. In the 1750s, the founders of Keene laid out all of the main lots so that the buildings would be set well back from the center of the highway. That decision set the tone for the development of downtown. At the north end of Main Street stands a large white church with a wedding cake spire. This is one of the most beautiful of New England's churches, and its location at the head of Central Square gives it a commanding presence.

On the west side of Main Street is the ochre-colored eighteenth-century *Wyman Tavern.* It was from this tavern that a contingent of Keene Minutemen departed to join in the Revolution on April 23, 1775, four days after the battle at Concord, Massachusetts. Prior to that, the first trustees' meeting of Dartmouth College was held here. The tavern is now a museum, furnished in the 1770–1820 period. It is open June 1 to Labor Day, Thursday through Saturday, 11:00 A.M. to 4:00 P.M., and the admission is $2.00. You'll find the Wyman Tavern at 339 Main Street in Keene (603–357–3855).

A short distance up the street from the tavern is Elliot Hall. The large brick building set back from the street is

Wyman Tavern

now part of Keene State College. In the spiral staircase of its front hall is a **Barry Faulkner mural,** depicting Central Square in Keene. Keene has several other examples of the work of this noted muralist whose work adorns the National Archives and Capitol Building in Washington, D.C. The lobby of Fleet Bank beside the church at the head of Central Square is decorated with his *Men of Monadnock* series. The Cheshire Medical Center on Court Street displays three smaller mural panels moved from another building, and the Keene Public Library has sketches made for his murals located elsewhere.

Other Barry Faulkner works are on display across lower Main Street in the **Archive Center of the Historical Society of Cheshire County.** Along with the Faulkner works, the museum's collections include a room dedicated to locally manufactured Hampshire pottery and examples of Keene and Stoddard glass. It is at 246 Main Street, Keene 03431 and is open Monday through Friday from 9:00 A.M. to 4:00 P.M. Call (603) 352–1875.

The *Arboretum and Gardens* at Keene State College are well described in a brochure that you can get free at the Mason Library on Apian Way, the pedestrian street that cuts through the center of the campus from Main Street. For some years, tree plantings have been planned to create a collection of specimen trees, and they now include a wide variety of exotics, several of which are at the far northern edge of their range. The booklet includes a map of the campus and silhouettes of leaf shapes to help you identify the species you'll see on a tour of the campus. For more information about the Arboretum, call the Plant Sciences Department at (603) 358–2544.

One of the state's most unusual "old house" museums is in this same neighborhood, next to St. Bernard's Church on Main Street. The *Horatio Colony House Museum* is not a home restored to one particular period, but the residence of a twentieth-century heir to a fortune that allowed him to live the life of a nineteenth-century gentleman of leisure. He traveled all over the world, collecting as he went, with a fine eye and highly cultivated tastes. The oriental art he brought back with him is at home in the 1806 Federal mansion amid the fine eighteenth- and nineteenth-century furnishings. Some of his collections are in glass cases in the ell, while other items are displayed as he lived with them. You will leave feeling that you have known this well-read, well-traveled, and generous gentleman who left his estate for others to enjoy. Open mid-May to mid-October, Tuesday through

Saturday, 11:00 A.M. to 4:00 P.M., and Saturdays year-round. Admission is free; park behind the church. The address is 199 Main Street in Keene; call (603) 352–0460.

Across the street is **176 Main,** a casual restaurant serving a wide selection of soups, sandwiches, and entrees. 176 likes to encourage microbreweries so the list of hard-to-find beers changes frequently. A terrace makes this casual restaurant particularly appealing during warm weather. At 176 Main Street, Keene 03431; telephone (603) 357–3100.

Not long ago, people in Keene used to go across the river to Brattleboro, Vermont, for a fine dinner; now Brattleboro people travel to Keene, especially since Italian-born chef Nicola Bencivenga has opened **Nicola's Trattoria**, with a menu of classic and innovative dishes based on impeccably fresh, high-quality ingredients. No short cuts here: The polenta is real, light in texture, and made the long, slow way instead of the quick-fix, heavy cornmeal mush served as polenta in too many places. The whole menu is enticing, but we usually order the specials just to see what he's created that day. Go on Saturday night for Osso Bucco, or any night for the Cioppino. The Risotto alla Milanese is superb—or choose any risotto special. It may be blended with perfectly cooked shrimp and pesto, or another equally delicious combination. Keene's our hometown, and this is our favorite place for dinner; it's at 39 Central Square, but you enter from Winter Street, beside the elegant 1858 brick courthouse (you can park behind the courthouse); (603) 355–5242. They're open for lunch and dinner, Tuesday–Saturday, and dinner entrees are $9.00–$16.00.

Keene's favorite place for a quick breakfast or lunch is **Timoleon's,** on Main Street, just south of Central Square. This is the sort of place where everyone calls the waitresses by their first names, and the menu has all of the old favorites. They are noted for chicken croquettes, meat loaf, and on Friday, codfish cakes. At 25–27 Main Street, Keene 03431; telephone (603) 357–4230.

Two for tea in downtown Keene are the **Celtic Cupboard** and **Heather's.** The former is a few steps off Main Street on Cypress Street and open every afternoon except Tuesday, with tea brewed in a china pot, fresh scones, and other teatime classics in a setting of bamboo furniture and pleasant Celtic music. Look here for British and Scottish gift and food specialties too; (603) 357–0188. Heather's is also a few steps off Main Street, opposite City Hall, at 28 Washington Street; (603) 357–7588. Their pastries are more varied—from cappuccino cheesecake to delicious almond cookies filled with raspberry jam—but your Earl Grey or herbal tea is served in giant paper cups. Shop here for locally produced specialty foods you won't find outside New Hampshire, and for fine imported pastas, preserves, and so on. Their selection of fresh-baked breads changes every day, and we've never met one that didn't invite a second slice. Don't overlook this place for breakfast or lunch; their sandwiches are stacked on their own bread, and the counter service is unfailingly with a smile. They're open 7:00 A.M. to 6:00 P.M. Monday–Friday, 8:00 A.M. to 4 P.M. on Saturday.

The **Fine Arts Center at Keene State College** has an active performance schedule (603–357–4041) and

Keene supports its own choral group, the Keene
Chorale. Their professional-quality concerts are held in
the spring and before Christmas and may include
sacred works such as masses and oratorios or operatic
choral selections. For a schedule of concerts call (603)
357–1534. During the summer, concerts featuring
popular bands are held on Wednesday evenings at the
bandstand in the common on Central Square from 7:00
to 8:30 P.M. (603–357–9829).

Swanzey, directly south of Keene, has maintained and
preserved three *covered bridges* over the Ashuelot River.
The following route will show you all of them. Leave
Keene on Route 10 (Winchester Street) and turn left on
Matthews Road just past the veterinary clinic. Go left at
the end and through the first of the bridges. When that
road ends, go left again and shortly join Route 32 at the
Potash Bowl (remember where this is—we'll get back to
it later). All this sounds complicated, but it's a distance of
only 3 to 4 miles. Go south on Route 32 to Carleton Road,
where you will find another bridge in a few hundred
yards. If it's early spring and the water is high, the bridge
may be closed, but you can drive down to watch the river
lapping at its floorboards. Return to Route 32 and
continue south to Swanzey Lake Road on your right.
Follow this winding road until it ends at a T. Go right,
and you'll come to West Swanzey. The third bridge is to
your left when you reach the crossroads at the top of the
hill. Go through it, then turn right, and you will come to
Route 10, which leads back to Keene (turn right).

Covered bridges did not originate in New England—
they were a common sight in the Alpine regions of
Europe for the same reasons early New Englanders built

Carleton Bridge

them. The roof protected floorboards and support timbers from the harsh weather and snow buildup that would weaken or break the bridge under its weight. Snow falling on the sloping roof would slide off, as it does on a house roof. The biggest job for road agents was shoveling snow *onto* the bridge so that sleigh runners could slide over them in the time of year when the sleighs replaced carriages and wagons for transport. (In New England, the term "road agent" means the person whose job it is to maintain roads. It does not refer to a highwayman, as it does in many other places.)

If you go left at Route 10 instead of right, you'll come to the *Swanzey Historical Museum* on your left, a newly opened building with some unusually interesting exhibits. Here you will find an operational Amoskeag steam fire pumper made in Manchester and a

Keene's Fireproof House

*F*red Sharby was afraid of fire. Two of the theaters he owned burned flat, and he had a terror of dying in a fire. So he tore down his house on the north side of Roxbury Street in Keene and built a new one, all of fireproof materials. Steel girders, stucco, plaster, and fireproof floor tiles, doors of solid metal, and a furnace enclosed in cement walls have indeed lasted to this day without a fire. Fred wasn't so lucky. He chose the night of November 28, 1942, to go to the Cocoanut Grove in Boston and died in that fire.

stagecoach. The museum is wheelchair accessible and is open June through October, Monday to Friday, 1:00 to 5:00 P.M., and Saturdays and Sundays, 10:00 A.M. to 6:00 P.M. on Route 12 in Swanzey; call (603) 352–4579 for more information.

For more than fifty years, the town of Swanzey has performed Denman Thompson's *The Old Homestead* at an open-air natural arena known as the ***Potash Bowl.*** Thompson's down-home plays, filled with moral lessons and country values, delighted New York theater audiences of the Victorian era. This play, performed each July, is a real period piece. Bring lawn chairs or blankets to sit on. Admission is $5.00 (603–352–0697).

Stonewall Farm is off Route 9, just outside of Keene, a demonstration farm with an active dairy herd. If you go between 4:30 and 6:30 P.M., you can watch the milking session, especially popular with children. Youngsters also enjoy the other animals that are kept close to the education center—a flock of chickens, a sow with a brood of piglets, goats, sheep, and a calf. The farm's two teams of Belgian draft horses can be seen grazing in the pasture or working on the farm as they plow, hay, or haul sap in the spring for the farm's sugarhouse. Stonewall Farm maple products are sold at the small gift shop in the education center. A 1.2 mile nature walk is self-guided, with the help of a sixteen-page booklet available at the trailhead. Special events include AutumnFest in late September, and a traditional Crafts and Fare in mid-November. For a complete schedule of events and programs, contact Stonewall Farm, 243 Chesterfield Road, Keene 03431; (603) 357–7278, fax (603) 357–6018.

Chesterfield Gorge shows the power of persistence. A relatively small brook has worn a deep gorge through the rocks here as it cascades from pool to pool for a distance of about ¼ mile. It is an easy hike, just over ½ mile, through a forest of beech and hemlock of unusual size. A small pavilion at the head of the trail contains information on the geologic history of the gorge's formation. A shady grove provides a good place for a picnic. The gorge is on Route 9, west of Keene.

Farther west, Route 63 crosses, leading south to Chesterfield and the entrance to ***Pisgah*** (pronounced "Piz-gee") ***State Park.*** The road to this wilderness preserve winds along the edge of a hill through mixed hardwood forests. There are no facilities in the 13,000 acres of this park, and camping is not allowed. Hiking and ski trails crisscross the area, which is a favorite with fishermen and hunters. Some of the trails connect with ***Road's End Farm Horsemanship Camp,*** on Jackson Hill Road, and you're welcome to hike on these trails as well. For ten weeks in the summer the camp is filled with girls sharing the experience of riding and caring for the camp's horses. In other seasons, experienced riders can call for reservations to enjoy these same trails and the views of Pisgah Park, Mount Monadnock, and even Mount Snow in Vermont. The farm's hilltop setting is unparalleled, and its gregarious owners hope to share it in the future by offering B&B accommodations. But for now, it's just for riders. Jackson Hill Road, Chesterfield 03443. Call (603) 363–4900.

If you follow it northward, Route 63 winds along the shore of Spofford Lake and into Westmoreland (pronounced with the accent on "west") and on through the settlement of *Park Hill,* a cluster of noteworthy early buildings, the likes of which are rare outside of Portsmouth or Exeter. The Meeting House is one of the state's earliest, built in 1762 with a façade and spire considered among the finest in their period of architectural design and detail. The Paul Revere bell was placed there in 1827. Around the church are several early homes, dating from as early as 1774.

Follow the signs off Route 63 in Park Hill to the Cheshire County Complex, a county-operated farm, where you can park at the top of the hill to enjoy one of the few walking trails along the banks of the Connecticut River. The *River Trail* overlooks steep banks in places, so you can actually look down onto the canopy of trees, a prime vantage for bird-watching. The trail is being extended, with signage pointing out natural features of the flora along the way.

Back at the farm, stop at the *Idea Garden*, a joint project of the farm and the Cheshire County Extension Service, where you can get ideas for your own garden from their one-acre plot, complete with arbor, pathways, and a small greenhouse.

Cheshire County's Extension Service is a very active one, with innovative programs to promote agriculture in the region and draw the public into farm activities. Check local events listings (on Friday *The Keene Sentinel* has a calendar for the coming week) for **Open Farm Days** during the summer, when a local farm is featured, and activities are planned for both adults and children. A popular attraction of these is the appearance of a van from the Granite State Dairy Promotion Board, dispensing unlimited quantities of free ice cream. The highlight of the agricultural year is the **Cheshire Fair** in early August, which, although it has a midway with rides, is still largely an agricultural event, with 4-II members showing their sheep and calves at the southern end of the fairgrounds and the lunch counter in the 4-H Building serving up old-fashioned homemade pies.

Route 63 winds past some of New Hampshire's finest and most fertile farmland, with meadows full of grazing cattle and views across the Connecticut River valley into Vermont. From mid-February until mid-April and from mid-September until the end of November you can stop for breakfast, lunch, or a snack at **Stuart and John's Sugar House.** It's best in late February and into March when the sap is running and the back room is filled with steam from the evaporators. The corn fritters and homemade doughnuts are delicious, and syrup comes in a full-sized milk pitcher that the waitress plunks on the table when she brings the menu. All you need to decide is what to pour it over.

If it's not breakfast or lunch time when you are passing by, try a maple sundae, frappé, or, in the fall, maple apple pie. This place isn't fancy; you sit on folding chairs at church supper-style tables. It's family style, family run, and a favorite low-cost Sunday outing for local families. Open weekends only, until 3:00 P.M., on Route 63 at Route 12 in Westmoreland (603–399–4486).

Northern Hills

Walpole looks down onto Route 12, and this picture-perfect village is a good place to stroll around and admire the beautifully preserved and maintained eighteenth- and nineteenth-century homes that encircle the green. On Sunday evenings during July and August, band concerts fill this grassy common with music and people.

The prosperity that built the many homes and public buildings in Walpole resulted from the building of a canal around the Great Falls of the Connecticut River in 1790, which allowed river traffic (water was the main means of moving goods in those days) to proceed past here to the north country. The heirlooms of many of these early families have found their way to the *Old Academy Museum.* Silk dresses with the kind of needlework that only prosperous women had the time to pursue have been preserved here along with furniture, tools, utensils and kitchenware, and a completely restored schoolroom from the original academy. Shaker furniture, and the original piano mentioned in *Little Women,* a gift to the Alcott sisters when they were living in Walpole, are just a few of the

Old Academy Museum

treasures that have been presented to the museum. Open from 2:00 to 4:00 P.M. Saturday and Sunday in July and August on Main Street in Walpole; call (603) 756–3449 for more information.

The chocolates made at ***Burdick's Chocolates*** by Swiss-trained Larry Burdick are the tops. Be sure to try one of their dark, white, or milk chocolate mice. The cafe at the shop serves hot chocolate, tea, or espresso and tempting pastry. Burdick's is open daily, 9:00 A.M. to 5:00 P.M., and until 6:00 P.M. on weekends. Main Street,

Walpole; (603) 756–3701 or (800) 229–2419 (to order chocolates by mail).

In a fine Federal home nearby is *Josiah Bellows House Bed and Breakfast*, a B&B with a unique story. When they first opened, they added the homey touch of a plateful of home-baked cookies on the nightstand. Guests couldn't get enough of them and began asking to have cookies sent to them by mail. Now the Bellows House Bakery is a full-blown business, providing boxes of cookies, brownies, and buttery shortbread by mail, and fresh muffins shipped by Federal Express. You can be sure the breakfast here is good, but they don't rest on their laurels as muffin-bakers supreme. They offer scones, too, and your choice of hot breakfast, cooked to order. The rooms all have private baths and are furnished in unfussy elegance with Persian rugs, antiques, and reproductions. They're on North Main Street at High Street; (603) 756–4250 or (800) 358–6302.

Few dairy farms in New Hampshire produce cheese, but a happy exception is *Boggy Meadow Farm* in Walpole, north of the intersection of Route 63 with Route 12. They sell Swiss and smoked Swiss cheeses in a small retail shop right at the farm where they are made on River Road. You'll find it from Route 12 by its discreet FARMSTEAD CHEESE sign; (603) 756–3300.

If you have a spare day and a sense of adventure, you could take any road out of Walpole and follow it until it ends in the dooryard of a farmhouse or bumps into Route 12A. The hillsides are covered with well-kept farms and are separated by lovely little hollows. The views over the valley are beautiful when you reach the hillcrests, most of which have been cleared for pasture land. North of Walpole, Route 123 heads into more hills, following the Cold River (*all* rivers here are cold; one wonders who decided that this one should be so honestly named). From the village of Drewsville, a road heads north toward Langdon, and in about a mile it passes New Hampshire's shortest covered bridge, only 36 feet long.

East of Alstead on Route 123A is another covered bridge and signs for ***Bascom's Maple Farms.*** From mid-March through the first week in April, while the sap runs, Bascom's evaporators, both the ultramodern osmo-separators and the old-fashioned steaming pans, produce syrup that will be shipped all over the world. It's a warm steamy place to be on a windy March day, and after you've watched sap becoming syrup, you can sample the traditional New England treat, sugar on snow. Actually, it's syrup on snow, and it makes a chewy candy that is always served with a dill pickle to balance its sweetness. Doughboys with syrup, maple pecan pie, and maple milk shakes are available here, and you can eat them at long tables covered with red-checked oilcloth. Bascom's sells syrup, maple cream, and candies throughout the year and will ship gifts for you as well. Maple treats are served in March and early April (call to make sure the run has begun), Saturday and Sunday, 11:00 A.M. to 5:00 P.M. Write Bascom's at R.R. 1, Box 137, Alstead 03602 or call (603) 835–2230 or 835–6361. Syrup and candy are sold during regular business hours on weekdays year-round.

PLACES TO STAY
IN THE MONADNOCK REGION
(ALL AREA CODES 603)

HANCOCK
The Hancock Inn, Main Street, 03449; 525–3318. Doubles are $106–$172, and it has a well-known dining room.

ANTRIM
Maplehurst Inn, Main Street, 03440; 588–8000. A comfortable country inn with a dining room. Doubles $60–$100.

PETERBOROUGH
Apple Gate Bed and Breakfast, 199 Upland Farm Road (at Route 123), 03458; 924–6543.

Peterborough Manor Bed and Breakfast, 50 Summer Street, 03458; 924–9832. $32–$45.

DUBLIN
Dubliner Bed and Breakfast, P.O. Box 151, 03444; 563–8700. Private baths at moderate prices near Keene.

RINDGE
Cathedral House Bed and Breakfast, 63 Cathedral Entrance, 03461; 899–6790. Full breakfast and moderate rates.

FITZWILLIAM
Hannah Davis House, Route 119, 585–3344. Full breakfast and private baths, $60–$115.

KEENE
The Carriage Barn Bed and Breakfast, 358 Main Street, 03431; 357–3812. A block from downtown shops, with three museums and an arts center within five minutes' walk, its location matches the quality of its rooms; only the rates are below average.

CHESTERFIELD
Chesterfield Inn, Route 9, 03443; 256–3211 or (800) 365–5515. Classy, pricey rooms in a fine, old home overlooking the Connecticut Valley.

ALSTEAD
Darby Brook Farm, Hill Road, 03602; 835–6624. Homey lodging on a small, working farm, open May–October.

PLACES TO EAT
IN THE MONADNOCK REGION
(ALL AREA CODES 603)

ANTRIM
Rynborn Restaurant, corner Routes 31 and 202, 03440; (603)588–6162. Lunch and dinner, American. Blues Lounge separate from dining room. Lunch and dinner Wednesday–Sunday, Sunday Breakfast from 7:30 A.M.

HILLSBOROUGH
Pat's Millview, Route 9, downtown, 03244; 464–3188. Homemade soups and sandwiches, chili. Breakfast and lunch until 2:00 P.M. (1:00 P.M. on Sunday) Wednesday–Monday. Inexpensive.

High Tide, Route 9, 03244; 464–4202. Fast-fried seafood, burgers, dogs, ice cream. Inexpensive.

PETERBOROUGH
Latacarta, Noone Mills, Route 202, 924–6878. The most truly eclectic menu we've encountered—not just a variety of cuisines, but skillfully blended. Lunch and dinner Tuesday–Saturday, with a 7:00 P.M. closing on Sunday.

Peterborough Diner, 10 Depot Street, 924–6202. It's the real thing, been there half a century, entrees $6.00–$12.00.

Donna's Riverside Bistro, Depot Square, 924–2002. Interesting salads and sandwiches at lunch; moderate prices.

JAFFREY
Michael's Jaffrey Manor, East Main Street, 532–8555. All-you-can-eat specials on Wednesday (fried clams), Thursday (prime rib), Friday and Saturday (seafood), at $10–$11.

RINDGE
Lilly's on the Pond, Route 202, Rindge; 899–3322. Innovative entrees, most $10–$12.

FITZWILLIAM
Fitzwilliam Inn, Route 119, 585–9000. Three-meals-a-day country dining room; entrees $13–$17.

KEENE
Bandido's Southwestern Grille, The Center of Keene, Emerald Street; 355–4366. Tex-Mex entrees, at $8.00–$11.00, range from ribs to Marguerita Chicken.

Mango's Cafe on Main, 81 Main Street, 358–5440. Pizzas, pastas and specials, entrees $7.00–$14.00.

Papagallos, Route 12 South, 352–9400. Family dining and interesting wood-fired pizzas, $8.00–$14.00.

Tolman's Table, The Center of Keene, Emerald Street; 355–8923. The ambience of a country farmhouse kitchen and budget-priced meals that range from meat loaf to veal Marsala. Fresh popovers are made with eggs from their own farm and come with all entrees, as do a salad of mixed greens and Indian pudding for dessert.

The Dartmouth-Sunapee Region

The Connecticut River flows through a broad, flat valley as it forms the border between New Hampshire and neighboring Vermont. Along its shores and up the hillsides that overlook it are sprawling farmlands: fields of corn, herds of cattle, truck farms, and family farms. Their massive barns and tall, round silos punctuate the landscape. These venerable homes were built by some of the earliest settlers in the valley.

The farms were not always so serene. The river was the major artery of travel for the Indians as well as the settlers, and the French and Indian War was fought along its banks. It was to educate Indians that Eleazer Wheelock founded a school that is now Dartmouth College. Its

The River's Ours 'Til It Floods

New Hampshire's northern border wasn't finally established until 1842, in the Webster–Ashburton Treaty, which finally set the international boundary with Canada. But the Vermont–New Hampshire line wasn't clear until a 1934 Supreme Court decision set it at the low water mark on the Connecticut River.

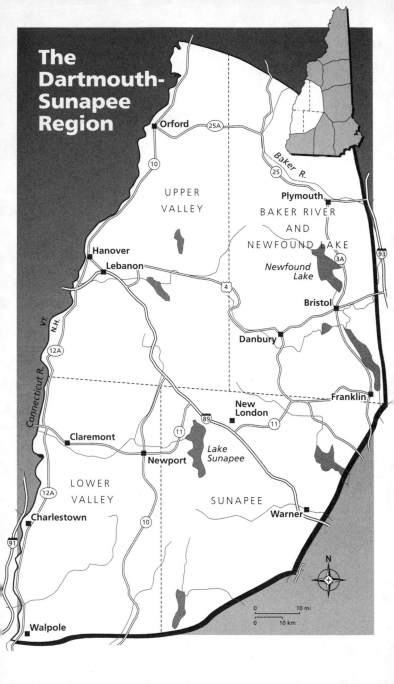

The Dartmouth-Sunapee Region

UPPER VALLEY

BAKER RIVER AND NEWFOUND LAKE

Newfound Lake

LOWER VALLEY

SUNAPEE

Lake Sunapee

Connecticut R.

VT.
N.H.

Baker R.

Orford

Plymouth

Hanover

Lebanon

Bristol

Danbury

Franklin

New London

Claremont

Newport

Warner

Charlestown

Walpole

0   10 mi
0   10 km

N

THE DARTMOUTH-SUNAPEE REGION'S TOP PICKS

The Fort at No. 4

Main Street National Historic District

Claremont Village Industrial District

West Claremont

Northstar Canoe Livery

Saint-Gaudens National Historic Site

Covered railroad bridges

Pollard's Mills Falls

Mt. Kearsarge Indian Museum

Nunsuch Dairy

Andover Historical Society Museum

Philbrick-Cricenti Bog

Luke Sunapee

Sunapee Historical Museum

The Fells

Baker Memorial Library

Hood Museum of Art

The Hanover Inn

Lower Shaker Village

Canaan Street

Profile Falls

Wellington State Park

Paradise Point Nature Center

Sculptured Rocks

The Quincy Bog

Town Pound

cultural influence and that of Colby-Sawyer College in nearby New London on the entire upper valley are significant, especially in the performing and fine arts.

To the east of the Connecticut River valley rise the gentle slopes of Mounts Sunapee, Kearsarge, and Cardigan—each about 3,000 feet in altitude—and other smaller mountains. The Appalachian Trail crosses the river on its way south, and nearly every mountain in the region, however small, has a trail to its summit.

Lakes dot the landscape. This region is a quiet part of the state, and even the interstate that bisects it hasn't changed that. In fact, from the point where I–89 leaves Concord until it arrives in Lebanon, at the Vermont border, there is almost no commercial activity visible along its sides, only miles of forest and farmland backed by mountain vistas.

The Lower Valley

The Fort at No. 4 was once the northwesternmost English-speaking village in the New World. This museum is an authentic reconstruction of the settlement founded there in 1740. It is New England's only living history museum of the period of the French and Indian War. Within its log stockade are furnished province houses and shops where costumed interpreters carry on the daily work of an isolated colonial village. Dinner is prepared in a huge open fireplace, candles are hand dipped, and wool and flax spun and woven. From the lookout tower, sentries kept watch over the river and valley for signs of attack by the

---

AUTHORS' FAVORITE ATTRACTIONS/EVENTS IN THE DARTMOUTH-SUNAPEE REGION

The Fort at No. 4, Charlestown (603) 826–5700

Saint-Gaudens National Historic Site, Cornish (603) 675–2175

Mt. Kearsarge Indian Museum, Warner (603) 456–2600

Hood Museum of Art, Hanover (603) 646–2808

Mt. Sunapee Ski Area, Sunapee (603) 763–2356

Dartmouth Winter Carnival, mid-February, Hanover (603) 795–2143

League of New Hampshire Craftsmen's Fair, early August, Sunapee (603) 224–3375

Yard Sale Day, late July, Charlestown (603) 826–5237

Fall Foliage Festival, early October, Warner (603) 456–2120

Dickens Holiday Celebration, early December, Hanover (603) 643–3115

Indians or the French. The skirmishes that took place here in those early years are re-created in full costume each year, and a cloud of smoke from musket fire hangs over the river as it did two-and-a-half centuries ago when, in 1747, it was besieged by a force of 400, but withstood the attack. This success resulted in the withdrawal of French forces to Canada and the beginning of English supremacy in northern New England. Of particular interest here is a working blacksmith shop, where a master smith creates the tools and utensils necessary for daily life and work on the frontier. A museum shop carries items of the period at extraordinarily reasonable prices. Open daily from Memorial Day through foliage season in October, from 10:00 A.M. to 4:00 P.M. every day except Tuesday.

Admission is $6.00 for adults and $4.00 for children ages six to eleven. The Fort at No. 4 is on Route 11 (Box 336), Charlestown 03603; call (603) 826–5700.

Charlestown's **Main Street National Historic District** is lined with distinguished homes, many dating from the early 1800s. It is almost a mile long, and fifty-two of its sixty-three buildings are historically important; ten of them date from the 1700s. The Unitarian Church and two of the houses were designed by Stephen Hassam, great-grandfather of the impressionist painter Childe Hassam, who often painted the Isles of Shoals. St. Catherine's Church has four signed Tiffany stained-glass windows. Stop at the office of the town clerk for an inexpensive booklet describing the history of each building.

Claremont's early settlers quickly saw the potential of the waterfalls in the Sugar River as it flows from Lake Sunapee to the Connecticut River. The first dam was built in 1767 for a grist and saw mill, and other plants soon followed, their machinery powered by the force from the 300-foot drop in the river as it passes through town. Mill buildings still dominate the center of Claremont, and you can learn how they once operated by following a walking tour of **Claremont Village Industrial District.** A free brochure available from the Chamber of Commerce on Tremont Square describes the original uses and evolution of various buildings, including mill workers' housing, owners' residences, shops, the foundry, weave shed, and others, each of which is marked on an accompanying map.

The manufacturing that created the massive mills along the Sugar River also created the wealth to build Claremont's imposing new City Hall in 1897, with its tall, prominent clock tower. On its third floor it boasted an opera house with the largest stage north of Boston. Although the **Claremont Opera House and Atrium** now has a separate handicapped-accessible entry, those who enter through the old building can enjoy the carved archway and oak paneling of the lower lobbies and public areas. The large opera house has a curved balcony and cast-iron-based seats; open one to see its unique reclining back. This outstanding example of public architecture of the past century still hosts varied performances on a regular basis. It is open for performances and from 9:00 A.M. to 5:00 P.M. on weekdays. Call (603) 542–1296 for hours or (603) 542–4433 for a schedule of events.

If the Boccia sisters ever tire of running their fruit store and lunch counter across the street from Claremont's City Hall, they can simply turn it into a museum and charge admission. At the **George Boccia Fruit Store,** drinks still come out of the big red Coke coolers in the middle of the floor or the refrigerated glass-front wall chests. A substantial collection of Coca-Cola advertising decorates the upper walls. A deli counter displays the day's salads, quiches, and soups—if you can't decide between the chicken salad and the equally delicious Portuguese sausage-and-rice salad, ask for a plate with a sampling of each. It will come with a thick slice of Rondy's bread; her sister Maria makes the salads and their mother tends the cash register from behind an old glass display case. A few small tables fill the front of the store; you can eat there and listen to the good-natured banter between the Boccias and their customers. The shop is at 66 Tremont Square, Claremont 03743; telephone (603) 542–9816.

If This Is Africa, Where Are the Lions?

*C*ontinental *plates are great travelers, but they don't tend to follow the admonition of today's ecotravelers to tread softly and leave no tracks. When these giant pieces of the earth's crust move, they leave lots of tracks; in fact, they leave pieces of themselves hanging about after they've left, which is what the African plate did after it bumped into Vermont. It left New Hampshire behind.*

This accounts for the obvious differences in landscape and the wholly different geologies of the two states. The Connecticut River covers the seam, except in one place, where you can actually see where Africa and North America meet. If you go to North Walpole, where the bridge crosses over a deep gorge and into Bellows Falls, Vermont, you can see the two different rocks join in the riverbank below you.

To the west, about 3 miles on Route 103, is the settlement of **West Claremont.** A road to the left leads across an old dam with mill foundations and again left to two historic churches. Union Church, a large, white clapboard building with curved windows, is the oldest Episcopal church building in New Hampshire. It is a surprise to see the oldest one this far inland—and this far from any present-day settlement. Its only neighbor, directly across the street, is St. Mary's Church, the first Roman Catholic church in the state, built between 1823 and 1825. The priest who established St. Mary's parish was the son of the Episcopal rector of Union Church across the street. The son had converted to Catholicism. The two men conducted a school for the children of West Claremont mill workers in the second floor of St. Mary's. Today, these vanguard churches stand alone, surrounded only by West Part Burying Ground, the settlement they once served long gone.

The Connecticut River flows peacefully between its wooded shores, perfect for traveling by canoe. You can rent a canoe at **Northstar Canoe Livery** in Cornish for half-day, full-day, or overnight trips on the Connecticut. The livery provides a shuttle that carries canoes and passengers upstream to put-ins either 4 or 12 miles distant. The 12-mile trip takes four to four-and-one-half hours; canoe rental and the shuttle are $17 per person. An overnight trip can be arranged so that you can camp on an island in the middle of the river. (You're still in New Hampshire, since New Hampshire owns to the normal high-water mark on the Vermont side. When it floods, Vermont owns the excess.) Northstar Canoe Livery is at Balloch's Crossing, Route 12A, in Cornish (603–542–5802).

The bridge across the Connecticut at Cornish is the **longest covered bridge in the United States.** (The longest in New Hampshire is at Bath; this one doesn't count since its other end is in Vermont.) Built in 1886, it traverses the river in two spans and has an unusual timber lattice-truss construction. At the turn of this century, Cornish was the home of a thriving colony of artists, writers, poets, and patrons who built or purchased summer homes around the studio of Augustus Saint-Gaudens. Italian terraced gardens surrounded old farmhouses, and the summer season's social life was one of wealthy bohemia.

The artists are gone, but the genius of the sculptor who attracted them to this retreat lives on in his beautifully situated home. His sculptures are displayed in the studios and galleries and throughout the grounds of the *Saint-Gaudens National Historic Site.* The gardens and grounds, lined with tall pine and hemlock hedges and delicate birch trees, are worth a visit in their own right. The original Stanford White bluestone base for the statue of Admiral David Farragut has recently been moved here from New York City where it was being damaged by pollution. The house, just as Mrs. Saint-Gaudens left it, is filled with artworks, each piece with some personal significance. A spirited house tour brings the family to life and lifts this site above the usual "home of a famous person" category. Sunday afternoon concerts in the summer bring musicians of all styles, along with music lovers carrying picnic baskets to the estate's shaded lawns. The house is open 8:30 A.M. to 4:30 P.M. daily from Memorial Day through late October; the grounds remain open until dusk. Admission is $2.00, free for ages under 16. Write to Saint-Gaudens National Historic Site, Box 73, Cornish 03745 or call (603) 675–2175.

Directly east of Claremont, Newport also preserves its late-nineteenth-century downtown. A busy rail line once connected these two towns, crossing the Sugar River twice on its way. The route is now a walking trail, level and smooth, covering 9.7 miles along the river. En route, it passes through two rare *covered railroad bridges,* the Chandler Station and Wrights. The former is clearly visible and both are accessible from Sugar River Drive, a dirt road that parallels the south bank of the river. From Claremont, take Broad Street (next to the park beside City Hall) to Chestnut and then left on Sugar River Drive. You can reach the path from Broad Street beyond the Chestnut Street intersection if you

Saint-Gaudens National Historic Site

want to walk or bike the whole distance, or you can pick up the path at any of several points where it crosses Sugar River Drive.

A cool place to while away a hot summer afternoon is **Pollard's Mills Falls**. Actually a long series of small falls on the South Branch of the Sugar River, the cascades work their way through several hundred feet of a granite chasm lined with boulders. A path through the trees at the top of the embankment brings you to the site of the old mills, their rough stone foundations very evident along the shore of the stream. Be sure to find the large square hole cut into the bedrock to anchor the machinery of the mill. To get to the Falls, follow Route 11 west of Newport about ½ mile and take a left onto Unity Road. Follow this for about a mile and then take a left onto Pollard's Mills Road. About ⁴⁄₁₀ mile farther, turn right at a Y in the road. Just around that corner is a parking area overlooking the falls. The path is to the left.

Sunapee

We have no intention of entering the historical dispute over the original meaning of *sunapee* in the Indian languages. It's a lovely region, in any language, with the mountain and lakes of the same name and the succession of smaller lakes between Mount Sunapee and Mount Kearsarge.

To the south lies Warner, with its ***Mt. Kearsarge Indian Museum.*** The museum's spirit is probably best summed up in the words of Chief Seattle in the late 1800s: "Every part of the earth is sacred to my people ... every shining pine needle, every sandy shore, every light mist in the dark forest ... we are part of the earth and it is part of us." The purpose of the museum is not so much to show the incomparable artifacts as to interpret the lifestyle through art and culture and to renew in all of us the positive relationship the Indians experienced between the earth and its people. It succeeds. The exhibits are the lifetime collection of Charles (Bud) and Nancy Thompson, who didn't want to have "a mausoleum of pickled artifacts," but rather a museum with a voice.

The voice is that of Indians. Except for the quotations, there are no written labels or signs in this beautifully displayed collection. Instead, a docent accompanies each visitor or group, explaining the displays focusing on those things that catch the visitor's interest. A museum shop sells authentic Indian handwork such as rugs, beadwork, and pottery, as well as books about various Indian tribes. Outdoors, a self-guided walk leads through two acres of native plants and trees used for medicine and food. Open May through October, Monday through Saturday, 10:00 A.M. to 5:00 P.M. and Sunday 12:00 noon to 5:00 P.M.; weekends, November to mid-December 12:00 noon to 5:00 P.M. Admission is $5.00 for adults and $3.00 for children ages six to twelve. Write Mt. Kearsarge Indian Museum, Kearsarge Mountain Road, P.O. Box 142, Warner 03278 (603–456–2600).

As you drive along New Hampshire's roads you will see a number of domesticated animals from the expected

Authors' Note

*O*ur high-school chum, Pat Hansen, now lives in Grantham, just north of Newport and quite close to the massive confines of Corbin Park. This huge, private game preserve is surrounded by a high fence, but exotic animals do escape from time to time, and wild boar are not an uncommon quarry for hunters in the adjoining woods. But none of us had ever seen one and had little idea of their size until we were looking at a collection of mounted animals one day in a museum and saw an enormous and unfriendly-looking wild boar. "Could you imagine getting one of those out of the woods?" I asked. "Not nearly so hard as getting me down out of the tree!" Pat rejoined.

cow to the exotic llama. *Nunsuch Dairy* in South Sutton raises Toggenburg goats. A small dairy by commercial standards, Nunsuch produces rondelles of goat cheese that are sought by the area's top restaurants. You can stop to visit this meticulously clean dairy and meet the enthusiastic owner, Courtney Haase. Prices on the cheese are phenomenally low and along with soft, fresh cheeses, Nunsuch has a Smoked Friar's Cheese. Pack a chunk of Nunsuch cheese for a lunch when you climb Mount Kearsarge, or take it on a picnic to a nearby shady roadside spot. Nunsuch Dairy is on Route 114, South Sutton 03221; call (603) 927–4176. (Courtney also sells gift packages of cheese on a goat-shaped board by mail: write Nunsuch Dairy, Star Route, Bradford 03221.)

In the Victorian-era railroad station at the village of Potter Place, the *Andover Historical Society Museum* has interesting collections, including an original Western Union Telegraph office. The building itself is intact, a fine example of the ornamented stations that once lined the tracks throughout New England. One of the highlights of the museum is a dugout canoe that is in very good condition; outside on the tracks are a caboose and a plow car used to clear the tracks during snowstorms. Open Saturday 10:00 A.M. to 3:00 P.M. and Sunday 1:00 to 3:00 P.M.

A short distance from Potter Place on Route 4 is the workshop of *The Village Whittler.* Wally Whitford specializes in deep relief carvings of local wildlife painted in colors so realistic that the trout appears to be jumping out of the wood panel. Loons are his most popular carving—you may have to wait for one of those, but he takes orders. Unique walking sticks begin at $5.00 in this tiny roadside shop. Hours are irregular, but you're pretty likely to find Wally there; or write to Box 177B, Route 4, South Danbury 03230; call (603) 768–5569.

The English House bed and breakfast in Andover is a little bit of Victorian Surrey transplanted. Its seven guest rooms, two of which are exceptionally large, have private baths, and two share a dormer sitting room with a window seat. This is only one example of the delightful architectural features of this meticulously restored turn-of-the-century home. Its British owners serve a classic full-course English breakfast with an international touch to the dishes, such as a Lebanese fruit compote. Proprietor Gillian Smith loves to share her considerable cooking talents with appreciative guests. Be sure to arrive in time for tea in the parlor.

Along with cooking and welcoming guests, Gillian offers classes in polymer clay jewelry making. Cross-country enthusiasts can ski out of the back yard onto a series of well-groomed trails maintained by neighboring Procter Academy. Rental skis are available only 200 yards away in the village. Ask for the Smiths' map of local antiques shops—five of the shops specialize in old books and one in old maps. In fact, The English House maintains a miniature travel office in the guests' lounge, with scrapbooks full of ideas for the guests' entertainment. Write The English House, P.O. Box 162, Andover 03216 or call (603) 735–5987.

La Meridiana in Wilmot is a family-owned restaurant dedicated to the foods of the chef's home in northern

Italy. Specialties include a salad of tender calamari, osso buco, gnocchi in a sauce so good that you'll be tempted to mop up the excess with the crusty Italian bread, and tender white veal with lemon served with lightly poached finocchi. The choice of desserts is equally varied and tempting: chocolate truffles, tiramisu, raspberry-chocolate cheesecake, zuppa inglese, cannoli, or a traditional chocolate sponge cake with ricotta filling. Prices on all courses are inexpensive to moderate, with two-thirds of the entrees under $10.00. The wine list is quite reasonably priced as well. An especially endearing feature is that they suggest sharing a pasta course, so those without a gargantuan appetite can split a dish of risotto, gnocchi, or agnolotti as a first course and still have room for the entrée to follow. La Meridiana is on Route 11 and Old Winslow Road in Wilmot; call (603) 526–2033.

New London is the home of **Colby-Sawyer College,** whose stately campus dominates the southern end of the town's main street. Throughout the school year theater and musical performances keep the local arts scene lively, and then a summer theater takes over the job with Broadway musicals. The town is a good center for hiking and skiing; hikers and walkers can choose from among eight or nine trails leading to or past such varied attractions as a cave, a quarry, cascades, a beaver pond, abandoned farms, and lovely mountain views. The **New London Barn Playhouse** really *is* in a barn, converted into a theater for a lively summer of musicals; (603) 526–4631.

The Philbrick-Cricenti Bog, a pond grown in with sphagnum moss, is located just out of the center of town. It is a fascinating nature reserve where you can observe the unique bog flora from wooden walkways, designed to protect both the fragile flora and your shoes. It's hard to see the trail sign from the road; look for the widened shoulder on the right after you pass Cricenti's Market. The trail is across the road.

Although spring-fed **Lake Sunapee** was a very popular resort area in the late 1800s, its shores have never been scoured by bulldozers or scarred by development. The only way to see the fine Victorian cottages nestled among the trees here is from the water. The **M/V Mount Sunapee II** takes passengers on an hour-and-a-half-long cruise along the 10-mile length of the lake, a tour made even more interesting by the intelligent and good-humored narration about the lake's history and lore. From the boat you can see Sunapee's three lighthouses, said to be the only ones on a New England lake. From mid-May to Columbus Day, the boat sails Saturday and Sunday at 2:30 P.M.; in addition, between mid-June and Labor Day it sails daily at 10:00 A.M. and 2:30 P.M. from Sunapee Harbor. For reservations write P.O. Box 345, Sunapee 03782 or call (603) 763–4030.

For a taste of the days of the grand hotels, dine aboard the **M/V Kearsarge,** a replica of the early lake steamers that brought guests from the train station to their lodgings. The *Kearsarge's* Victorian interior sets the stage for a buffet supper served during the summer sailings from Sunapee Harbor at 5:30 and 7:45 each evening. For reservations call (603) 763–5477.

Until the 1930s, the Woodsum family operated a fleet of steam passenger ships on Lake Sunapee. The **Sunapee**

M/V *Mount Sunapee II*

Historical Museum displays the pilot house of one of these rescued when the 70-foot SS *Kearsarge,* built in 1897, sank in 1935. Memorabilia of that golden age, including the handmade steam engine of a horseless carriage made in Newport in 1869, a milk delivery wagon, an 1824 fire pumper, an intact eighteenth-century dugout canoe, shop signs, and even a wooden water pipe, fill the museum. Plans are under way to restore the Woodsum Bros. machine shop. The museum is open 1:00 to 5:00 P.M. Tuesday through Sunday and 7:00 to 9:00 P.M. Wednesdays during July and August; weekends only in the spring and fall. It is at the landing in Sunapee Harbor; telephone (603) 763–2101.

Across the street at **Bob Skinners** and at **Alden of Sunapee,** kayaks, canoes, and paddle boats are available for daily or hourly rental. Each place has only one canoe, so making a reservation is wise. Call the former outfitter at (603) 763–9880 and the latter at (603) 763–3177.

Along with its lake, Sunapee is known for its mountain, where the Mount Sunapee State Park has camping, a chairlift that operates in the summer as well as for skiers at the ski area in the winter.

New England Handicapped Sports Association at Mt. Sunapee offers a unique opportunity for people who may have thought it was impossible for them to enjoy the ski slopes, as well as a chance for active skiers to share their sport with people of all ages and with any number of disabilities. Mt. Sunapee offers lift tickets, and the association provides adaptive equipment and the expertise. Volunteers act as instructors, guides, blockers (e.g., to alert other skiers to the approach of a blind skier) or simply to greet newcomers and get them started. NEHSA has its own wheelchair-accessible lodge, and new skiers will enjoy learning on their own private slope. To learn more, to become a volunteer, or to join the program, call NEHSA at (800) 628–4484.

Late in the nineteenth century, New Hampshire promoted the re-use of abandoned farms as summer homes for the wealthy. John Hay, Secretary to Abraham Lincoln, acquired **The Fells** in Newbury, at the southern tip of Lake Sunapee, in 1888. After his death, his son Clarence and his wife created extensive gardens on the property overlooking the lake. The rock garden covers both sides of a gently falling ravine and includes a stone Japanese

OFF THE BEATEN PATH

lantern presented to Hay for his role in the Treaty of Portsmouth in 1905; a small stream flows through the ravine into a rock-lined lily pond before continuing into the forest below. The rose and perennial beds are in more formal terraced gardens, and an easy trail to the lake features placards with nature notes. On Route 103A between New London and Newbury, The Fells is open 10:00 A.M. to 6:00 P.M. weekends from late May through Labor Day. Contact NH Division of Parks and Recreation, P.O. Box 295, Newbury 03255; telephone (603) 763–2452.

Newbury's *Center Meeting House* was originally built about 1821, but was disassembled and rebuilt on its present site in 1832. A Bulfinch-inspired design, it has a unique interior arrangement; the box pews of the congregation face the entry doors (which would surely discourage late arrivals). The finely executed woodwork of the pulpit is supported by four columns and reached by a double staircase. Sunday services during July and August are at 11:00 A.M.

Railroads were important to the future of small towns when the line to Newbury was built in 1871. To complete it, the engineers had to excavate a massive trench, the *Newbury Cut,* through a solid granite hilltop using nitroglycerin to blast and strong backs to move the rubble, a process that took a year. Although the trains haven't run since 1961, you can get to the still-impressive cut in a leisurely twenty-minute walk along the old railbed, now a level birch-lined path alongside a marsh. Park at the town landing, just across the Route 103 intersection from the Meeting House, and look for the wide trail behind the small shopping center.

Upper Valley

The town of Hanover and ***Dartmouth College*** are clustered around a large green, decorated in winter by a giant ice sculpture if the weather cooperates. Overlooking this from a slight hill are the white buildings of the original college. Two of the remaining sides are lined with red brick college buildings, among them Baker Library. The south side is divided between the Hanover Inn and the Hopkins Center for the Performing Arts. In and around that quadrangle lies an amazing wealth of art.

In the basement of ***Baker Memorial Library*** is a series of frescoes completed in 1934 by the Mexican artist José Clemente Orozco. A free brochure describing the frescoes is available at the central desk. They are powerful, and since their recent cleaning and restoration, true to their original brilliant colors. They were quite controversial in the 1930s but are now appreciated as a rare art treasure. Even less well known is the Hickmott ***Shakespeare Collection,*** also housed at Baker Library in the special collections room, open 8:00 A.M. to 4:30 P.M. Monday through Friday. The collection includes all four of the folio editions, close to forty quarto editions, all of the pre-1700 editions of *Macbeth,* and many other early editions. In the library's treasure room is Daniel Webster's set of John James Audubon's *Birds of America* in a folio first edition, more than 150 titles of incunabula (works printed before 1501), a 1439 Bible, and a collection of more than 200 volumes illustrating the art of fine book binding.

Adjoining the Hopkins Center is the new *Hood Museum of Art,* containing galleries for collections of American, European, African, Indian, and ancient art. The collection of Assyrian reliefs from the ninth century B.C. is rivaled in New England by only one other series. At the other end of history, the Hood is one of the very few American museums to own the entire suite of Picasso's Vollard etchings. There are Roman mosaics, paintings of the Italian Renaissance, baroque period, and Hudson River school, and representative pieces from every major style and period. Traveling exhibits often incorporate pieces from Dartmouth's own collections.

In 1991 the museum acquired the most comprehensive collection of Melanesian art in the country. Nearly 1,000 objects from Papua New Guinea and Vanuatu, ranging in size from miniatures to monumental works more than 8 feet tall, form a collection both comprehensive and rich in detail. Even with its new building, the museum cannot display everything, so inquire if you are interested in a particular subject. Temporary special exhibitions change twice each Dartmouth term. Open all year, Tuesday through Saturday 10:00 A.M. to 5:00 P.M. and Sunday 12:00 noon to 4:00 P.M. You can write for information to The Hood Museum, On the Green, Hanover 03755, or call (603) 646–2808.

The *Hopkins Center* is as broad in its offerings of performing arts as the Hood is in the fine arts. Telephone (603) 646–2422.

The Hanover Inn is an institution almost as revered as Dartmouth College itself. Whenever the inn changes so much as a carpet, some old grad notices and comments.

That has not stopped the inn from undertaking renovations to keep it up to date with modern amenities such as phones with modem ports. As the oldest continuously operated business in New Hampshire, the inn treads a careful balance between maintaining its historical flavor and providing luxurious accommodations and service that anticipates every need. Rooms are elegant, some with real marble baths. In the Daniel Webster Room's carpeted pink and gray Edwardian setting, Chef Michael Gray presents a menu as understated and elegant as the decor. Dinner may begin with an appetizer of delicately smoked tender scallops, then proceed to veal or a tuna steak served with shrimp dumplings. Flavors and textures are perfectly balanced in dishes that blend the nuances of a variety of cuisines. In short, the dining room is worthy of the hotel. Open for lunch and for dinner, Tuesday through Sunday, its address is: On The Green, Hanover 03755; telephone (800) 443–7024.

If you are a celebrity watcher, you can get the autograph of those performing or speaking at the Hopkins Center by waiting in the corridor that connects it with the inn. They all stay at the inn and use this private lower-level passageway before and after appearances. Expect to pay well for rooms in this top-rated hotel, but also expect to get your money's worth. Write The Hanover Inn, On the Green, Hanover 03755; call (603) 643–4300 or (800) 443–7024.

In an unimposing corner storefront facing the common in nearby Lebanon, **Sweet Tomatoes Trattoria** has quickly become a mecca (or should we say Bologna?) for lovers of real Italian food. From their wood-fired oven emerge roasted eggplant for caponata, roasted mushrooms for antipasto, and roasted chicken and peppers for several dishes, not to mention an array of pizzas, many topped with wood-roasted vegetables. We have, in the past year, ordered everything on their substantial menu at least once, from the linguine with calamari to the marinated chicken grilled with herbs, and our favorite is always the one that's just been set in front of us. Entrée prices are under $10.00 and wines are sold by the glass or by the bottle. Portions are generous, service personal, and the atmosphere upbeat and relaxed. Sweet Tomatoes is at One Court Street, Lebanon 03766; telephone (603) 448–1711.

The **Lower Shaker Village** at Enfield, while not as extensive as the one at Canterbury, is of special interest for its stone architecture. The largest Shaker dwelling house in existence, four-and-one-half stories tall, is now the Shaker Inn, which has a restaurant downstairs and inexpensive guest accommodations in the austere upper floors. These rooms have the sparse simplicity and built-in cabinets that are hallmarks of Shaker design. Write The Shaker Inn, Enfield 03748 or call (603) 632–5466.

The museum portion is best known for its herb gardens and for the regular series of workshops in Shaker arts, industries, and gardening held there throughout the year. In early June, a Festival of Shaker Crafts and Herbs features plants, herbal and Shaker crafts, demonstrations, and programs on herb gardening and cooking. Open June 1 to October 15, Monday through Saturday, 10:00 A.M. to 5:00 P.M., Sunday 12:00 noon to 5:00 P.M., and weekends only through the winter. It's on Route 4A in Enfield; call (603) 632–4346 for more information.

Northwest from the village of Canaan is the unusual settlement of **Canaan Street.** The main, and only, street is lined on both sides with a mile of distinguished white homes and churches. These date from as early as 1794. Behind the single row of homes on the east is a lake, and in the other direction is a sweeping view over the valley to the Green Mountains of Vermont. Wide lawns surround the homes, and the broad street is lined with maples and stone walls. The entire scene, so unexpectedly encountered, seems to have been dropped there from the last century. The last house on the left is **The Inn on Canaan Street,** one of the quietest and most lovingly managed of New Hampshire's many small inns. Breakfast here always features fresh baked scones or muffins. Rooms are large, bright, and comfortable; prices are moderate. Write to them at Box 92, Canaan Street, Canaan 03741; or call (603) 523–7310.

On Route 118, 3 miles from the center of Canaan, Dan Allen of **Highland Meadow Wood Carvings** creates wood sculptures, including 12-foot-long life-size moose, and larger-than-life animals, such as the appealing squirrel in the front yard. A 3-foot garden gnome, reading a book while perched on a mushroom, is about $65, while smaller figures are less. There is no sign, but look for a pile of logs across from the house and examples of Allen's work on the lawn. Write to him at RFD 2, Box 19, Canaan 03741 or call (603) 523–7291. After you've been here you'll recognize his work adorning area businesses.

Baker River and Newfound Lake

New Hampshire is filled with stone profiles, and although none rivals the fame of the Old Man of the Mountain in Franconia Notch, each has its degree of local renown. Some require a great deal of imagination or at least a view from the right spot to distinguish. **Profile Falls,** 2½ miles south of Bristol on Route 3A, demands both imagination and the right view, but even without spotting the profile, the falls themselves are well worth the short walk. Turn off Route 3A to the east (left if you're traveling south) just before the bridge with the small sign for the falls. A short distance down that road is another small sign and a pull-out area on the right, but it is steep and slippery, so we suggest parking along the road just before the sign. Follow the road to the trail or follow the snowmobile trail, which also leads to the base of the falls. The drop is about 40 feet over a broad ledge, and the profile is supposed to be at the foot of the falls in silhouette against the white water. On hot days, local boys can often be found jumping from the high rocks on the right into the pool at the base of the falls. We don't recommend that you try this.

North of Bristol on Route 3A is a picnic area maintained by the Rotary Club, in a grove of pines. Shortly past this a road leads to West Shore Road, which hugs the shore of Newfound Lake and offers lovely views of the lake and mountains. Along the road, on a point of land surrounded by the unusually clear waters of the lake, is one of New Hampshire's finest and perhaps least known beaches. **Wellington State Park** has a fine sandy beach under tall pines, so you can choose sun or shade and still be at the water's edge. You can't launch boats from the park, but you can put in canoes or small sailing craft easily. It is a busy, friendly park with plenty of beach and water, so it never seems crowded. It's open 9:00 A.M. to 8:00 P.M. on weekends from Memorial Day to the last week of June and for the two weeks after Labor Day. During the rest of the summer it's open daily from 9:00 A.M. to 8:00 P.M.

At the northern end of the lake, between the attractive village of Hebron and Route 3A, is the *Hebron Marsh Wildlife Sanctuary.* You can park down the dirt road just before the red cottage while you visit the diverse wildlife habitats of freshwater marsh, open fields, and the banks of the Cockermouth River. Follow signs to the southwest corner of the field to find the short trail leading to the observation tower. From here you can look out over the marsh and see wood ducks, buffleheads, pie-billed grebes, great blue herons, osprey, beaver, and perhaps moose and loons. Songbirds abound, and the trail through the fields gives a closer view of the wildflowers.

Only 1¼ miles down the road is the *Paradise Point Nature Center* (look sharp to find its sign on the downhill side of the road next to the driveway). In addition to the trails through an unspoiled lakeshore of coniferous forest, the center includes hands-on exhibits, a library, bird-viewing area, and a fascinating audio-aided exhibit demonstrating the various calls of the loon. A full schedule of naturalist programs is offered, including a sunrise canoe trip. Before walking the trails, be sure to pick up the free visitors guide, with descriptions of the natural history and inhabitants of the area. Try to spot the tupelo tree, rarely found in New England, as you walk alongside the swamp on the Elwell Trail. Its horizontal branches are covered in brilliant red leaves in the fall. The center is open weekends 10:00 A.M. to 4:00 P.M. in the spring and fall and daily 10:00 A.M. to 5:00 P.M. from the last week in June to Labor Day. There is no admission fee, but the Audubon Society, which operates the center, is always grateful for donations to help them continue their work of acquiring and protecting natural habitats. Write Audubon Society of New Hampshire, North Shore Road, East Hebron 03232 or call (603) 744–3516.

Going west from Hebron through Groton, a road leads to *Sculptured Rocks.* About a mile from the turnoff, watch for a signpost, although the sign may not be there during the off-season. You'll see a parking area on the left, and the chasm is on the right side of the road. The river here has carved its way under granite boulders, leaving only the crowns of some and forming giant potholes in others that appear to have been the work of a giant ice cream scoop. Below the bridge a trail leads past falls, pools and huge moss-covered boulders, culminating in a sheer rock cliff on one side. Notice the full-grown trees on the side walls with their roots gripping the walls like fingers.

The back road through Groton and North Rumney is a seldom-traveled alternative to Route 3A. The town of Rumney sits off Route 25, spread around a central common. Quilt enthusiasts should stop at the Calico Cupboard for a wide selection of fabrics, supplies, and books (603–786–9567).

Quincy Road, which goes off the far end of Rumney's village green, will take you to **The Quincy Bog.** Exactly 2 miles from the village green you will see stone pillars on either side of a small road to the left. Down this road 1/10 mile there is another left, which ends shortly at the bog entrance. Nature trails and a viewing deck offer a look at rare bog plants and a wetland ecosystem different from those of shores and marshes. The best months to see the bog plants in bloom are May and June.

On the way to Quincy bog you will pass the most unusual **Town Pound** in the state. While pounds were usually made of four sturdy stone walls, forming a square, with a gate on one side, the townspeople of old Rumney took advantage of a geological feature as interesting as the pound itself. Huge boulders, which appear to have fallen from the cliffs above, lie in a great tumble. Two of them form protected cavelike areas, and two others form straight walls. By adding only one-and-a-half sides and a gate, the town created a fine enclosure for stray animals, one that even offered shelter from rain and wind. Climb through the space in the center of the back and you'll find a trail through an arch formed by two huge boulders. You can climb farther and wander amid these granite giants. The pound is a fascinating combination of natural and human history. You'll see one wall of the pound directly across the road from the immense boulder that sits almost in the road.

Leaving Rumney on Main Street you will pass an extraordinary garden where visitors are welcome. **Mr. Jacquith's Garden** seems to be in bloom all the time, with a succession of flowers set in showy beds along the road. A place of visual delight, this work of one man rivals the loveliest show gardens anywhere. There is no admission fee, but you'll see a box for donations to help with the expense of replacing plants, and you'll probably want to add something to it. Although Mr. Jacquith is no longer living, his son and daughter-in-law, who run the plant nursery next door, have maintained his garden. At the nursery is a charming small perennial garden, and they sell herb and flower plants from their greenhouse, and fresh vegetables at their farmstand.

The road past these gardens leads to Stinson Lake. Along the way is the *Mary Baker Eddy House.* The founder of the Christian Science faith lived here in the early 1860s. The house is open Tuesday through Saturday 10:00 A.M. to 5:00 P.M. and Sunday 2:00 to 5:00 P.M. May through October. From here a guide will also take you to another Eddy home in North Groton. The road, which turns to gravel, continues to climb through the woods. Watch for a waterfall to the left just as you cross a bridge. Farther on, as you top the ridge, you will have sweeping views into the White Mountain National Forest, just a teaser for the views you will have as you continue north.

If your taste for travel doesn't run to dirt roads you can go north from Rumney through the National Forest along Route 118 or take Route 25 to Plymouth, a short distance away. On the way to Plymouth on this route you'll see *Glory Jean's,* a shiny O'Mahoney diner built in 1954. It's the real thing inside, too, with '50s tunes on the jukebox and diner favorites like hot turkey sandwiches, meat loaf, bread pudding, and homemade pies. Call the diner at (603) 786–2352.

Not far south of Glory Jean's is **The Crabapple Inn Bed & Breakfast,** in a beautiful 1835 Federal-style home. As well restored inside as out, the inn provides such luxuries as a canopied four-poster bed in a room whose private bathroom is large enough to be a guest room. Handmade quilts, antique furnishings, mountain views, herb and perennial gardens, and the choice of an elegant dining room or a bricked terrace as a setting for breakfast are just a few of the touches here. The rates are a little higher than at many B&Bs ($70–$105 per couple), but this is an elegant and comfortable home. Write to the inn at RR 4, Box 1955, Plymouth 03264, or call (603) 536–4476.

PLACES TO STAY
IN THE DARTMOUTH-SUNAPEE REGION (ALL AREA CODES 603)

CLAREMONT
Goddard Mansion Bed and Breakfast, 25 Hillstead Road, 543–0603 or (800) 736–0603. Ten beautifully decorated guest rooms in a 1905 summer mansion, with Tiffany chandelier and fine architectural details; doubles $65–$105, including breakfast.

CHARLESTOWN
Maple Hedge Bed and Breakfast, 355 Main Street, 03603; 826–5237. Part of the National Historic District, with antiques-furnished guest rooms, private baths, and moderate prices.

NEWPORT
Newport Motel, Routes 11 and 103, 03773; 863–1440 or (800) 741–2619. A tidy, well-managed motel with air-conditioning, pool, and moderate rates.

NEW LONDON
New London Inn, Main Street, 863–1440 or (800) 741–2619. Nicely restored rooms overlooking the center of town and the college campus. The

dining room offers a varied and interesting menu at moderate-to-high prices.

Jonathan Hunting House Bed and Breakfast, Shaker Road, 03257 (off Route 11); 526–9339. Quiet lodgings in a fine old home in well-tended gardens.

SUNAPEE
Haus Edelweiss, Maple Street, 763–2100 or (800) 248–0713. Homey, comfortable rooms and a hearty German (or American if you prefer) breakfast at budget prices.

For lodging reservations in the Sunapee area, call (800) 258–3530. To rent a lakeside cottage for a week, call Susan Morel & Company in New London; 526–2436.

ENFIELD
Mary Keane House, Lower Shaker Village, 03748; 632–4241; Elegant Victorian B&B with suites and private baths. Moderate to expensive.

Shaker Farm B&B, Route 4A, 03748; 632–7664 or (800) 613–7664. Large rooms with private baths, from $65.

LYME
Loch Lyme Lodge, 70 Orford Road, 03768; 795–2141 or (800)

423–2141. An old-fashioned family summer camp, with cabins on a pond and canoeing.

BRISTOL
Victorian Bed and Breakfast Inn, 16 Summer Street (Route 104E), 744–6157.

BRIDGEWATER
The Inn on Newfound Lake, Route 3A, 03222; 744–9111.

PLACES TO EAT
IN THE DARTMOUTH-SUNAPEE REGION (*ALL AREA CODES 603*)

ANDOVER
The Potter Place Inn, Routes 4 and 11, Potter Place, 735–5141. Dinner every night and Sunday brunch of Eggs Benedict and other treats. Guest rooms with private baths, too.

NEW LONDON
Peter Christian's Tavern, 186 Main Street, 526–4042. Hearty food and sandwiches, accompanied by a good range of microbrews; open every day.

SUNAPEE
The Anchorage, Sunapee Harbor; 763–3334. An informal place for breakfast or lunch, overlooking

the lake. Slips available if you arrive by boat.

HANOVER
Cafe Buon Gustaio, 72 South Main Street, 643–5711. Italian, open Tuesday–Saturday for dinner, entrees $7.00–$16.00.

Peter Christian's Tavern, 39 South Main Street, 643–2345. A tavern atmosphere, serving large sandwiches, generous entrees at budget prices; open every day.

PLYMOUTH
The Main Street Station, Main Street, 536–7577. Newly opened as we write, but getting rave reviews from local residents for its traditional menu and moderate prices.

The Italian Farmhouse, US Route 3, south of Plymouth; 536–4536. It's really a New Hampshire farmhouse, its kitchen and parlor transformed into dining rooms, but the restaurant in it is decidedly Italian. Interesting pasta dishes are budget priced, beginning at $6.00.

BRISTOL
Cliff Lodge Country Dining, Route 3A (on Newfound Lake), 744–8660. Dinner and Sunday brunch overlooking the lake and mountains. Moderate.

The Lakes and Foothills

North of the Merrimack Valley and the seacoast regions lies an area of rolling farmlands and small mountains. The northernmost of these are the foothills of the White Mountains beyond.

In the center lies Lake Winnipesaukee, an enormous body of water surrounded by several other sizable lakes. The southern shores of Winnipesaukee are covered with popular tourist paths and filled with man-made "attractions" and cheek-by-jowl resorts. While there are some lovely, quiet pockets in this area, it is generally too well known and too heavily trodden to be of interest in this book.

Instead, we shall explore the eastern shore of Lake Winnipesaukee and other lakes east of I–93 and the mountains and forests that border them. Ossipee, Wentworth, Squam, Silver, and Province lakes are joined by innumerable smaller ones providing reflecting pools for some of the state's prettiest villages. We won't name or take you past all of them, so you should explore the back roads to discover some of them for yourselves. Country inns, covered bridges, rock-lined brooks, and old farms lie along back roads here, and at the crossroads are villages that date from the earliest days of the colony.

The Lakes and Foothills

THE
SANDWICHES

Ossipee Lake

NEW HAMPSHIRE
MAINE

Squam Lake

SQUAM

Holderness

OSSIPEE

Meredith

Ossipee

Lake Winnipesaukee

Lake Wentworth

Wolfeboro

Winnisquam Lake

Laconia

WINNIPESAUKEE

Alton

Farmington

N

0   10 mi
0   10 km

THE LAKES AND FOOTHILLS' TOP PICKS

New Hampshire Farm Museum

Museum of Childhood

Wentworth Park

Wright Museum

Clark House Museum Complex

M/V **Doris E**

Abenaki Tower

The Effinghams

Freedom Historical Society

Madison Boulder

Snow Village Inn

Bike the Whites

White Lake State Park

Summer Brook Fish Farm

The Old Country Store

Sandwich Historical Society Museum

Sandwich Notch

The Corner House

Science Center of New Hampshire

Red Hill Inn

Winnipesaukee

Memories of New Hampshire's early agriculture are displayed and used at the ***New Hampshire Farm Museum*** on Plummer's Ridge, just north of Milton. Housed in the state's best-preserved series of connected farm buildings (the house and barn are connected by a series of buildings and sheds to facilitate winter access and farm chores), the museum began as a simple collection of early implements. In addition to the house and barn (the latter is filled with fascinating old tools and equipment) there are blacksmith and cobbler shops. Next door, the Plummer homestead, an equally fine set of connected farm buildings, has recently become part of this museum as an active, working farm. Together, they give a rare picture of nineteenth-century farm life. Special weekend events illustrating early farm life include days featuring herbs, dairy farming, fibers, farm animals, and other subjects. The second Saturday in August is Old Time Farm Day, with more than sixty demonstrations of farming skills and crafts. Open mid-June to Labor Day, Tuesday through Saturday 10:00 A.M. to 4:00 P.M., Sundays 12:00 noon to 4:00 P.M., and on weekends for the same hours in the fall. Admission is $5.00 for adults, $1.50 for children. Write New Hampshire Farm Museum, Route 125, P.O. Box 644, Milton 03851 or call (603) 652–7840.

For most of the nineteenth century, ***Wakefield Corner*** was an important stop on the route north, but then it lost its position to Sanbornville's rail junction. Since then, it has stayed so close to its nineteenth-century appearance that the entire village has been named a historic district. Its white wooden houses sit in gracious fence-encircled

---

AUTHORS' FAVORITE ATTRACTIONS/EVENTS IN THE LAKES AND FOOTHILLS

New Hampshire Farm Museum, Milton (603) 652–7840

Madison Boulder, Madison

Science Center of New England, Holderness (603) 968–7194

M/V Mount Washington, Center Harbor (603) 366–BOAT

M/V Doris E, Wolfeboro and Center Harbor (603) 366–2628

Strawberry Festival, late June, Laconia (603) 524–8813

Old Time Farm Day, mid-August, Milton (603) 652–7840

Meredith Chowder Festival, early October, Meredith (603) 293–INFO

---

yards, and features such as the hay scales and horse trough are still standing. A Rails-to-Trails project is in progress, converting the former railbed into a hiking and biking path from Wakefield to Wolfeboro.

The innkeepers of **The Wakefield Inn** have prepared a booklet describing the architecture and the buildings in town, which they lend to guests who wish to take a walking tour. That's only one of the reasons for staying at this three-and-a-half-story Federal-style inn. The rooms are large, airy, and beautifully decorated, all with private bath. Historical features such as original window glass, a three-sided fireplace, and Indian shutters make the inn as interesting as it is hospitable; guests enjoy gathering to share their day's travel experiences around the glass-fronted woodstove. Throughout the inn, walls are decorated with fine needlework and owner Lou Sisson's quilting. She offers a number of special quilting weekends in the spring and winter, with classes in the inn, well-prepared meals (she's an accomplished chef, too) and the company of fellow quilters. Ask for a schedule of these programs, which are graded according to the experience level of the participants. Dinner is also served to nonquilting guests by prior reservation. In a business where innkeepers tend to burn out quickly, it's nice to meet a couple who still look forward to the arrival of each guest after a dozen years as innkeepers. Write the inn at Mt. Laurel Road, Route 1, Box 2185, Wakefield 03872; telephone (603) 522–8272 or (800) 245–0841.

A few doors up the street is the *Museum of Childhood.* Two sisters, Marjorie Banks and Elizabeth MacRury, have collected dolls and toys both at home and on their frequent foreign travels. When the collection threatened to engulf their home, they purchased a house a few doors away, and the museum was born. More than 3,000 dolls, from puppets to clothespin dolls, inhabit the rooms, along with teddy bears, sleds, and a *complete* 1890s schoolroom. The collectors, who are happy to accompany visitors and bring these bits of childhood memories alive, are as delightful as the collection. Everyone leaves smiling, especially children, who can't resist the stories. "Sara is visiting her grandmother in Tuftonboro today, but she won't mind your looking in her room," Elizabeth assures a young visitor. Open May through October, Wednesday through Monday 11:00 A.M. to 4:00 P.M., except Sunday 1:00 to 4:00 P.M. The Museum of Childhood is on Mt. Laurel Road in Wakefield; call (603) 522–8073 for more information.

Almost next door to the inn is a unique shop, the *Dutch Boutique,* owned by a couple from the Netherlands and featuring a charming mixture of Dutch imports and New Hampshire–made products. He's a retired doctor

The Wentworth Wives

*I*t's easy to confuse the three Wentworths, all of them Royal Governors, and all with a habit of marrying each others' widows, which muddies the waters even more. But Benning, the best known of them, married his housekeeper, much to the shocked surprise of his guests, at a dinner party celebrating his sixtieth birthday. He chose this occasion to announce his intentions, introduce his new love to New England society, and celebrate the wedding itself, catching the rector of St. John's Church, one of the dinner guests, quite by surprise as well.

and a skilled Hingelope artist; she's a black-and-white photographer. Hingelope is an intricate form of country painting, somewhat similar to German and Scandinavian decorative painting. Up the road, at the intersection of the village's main street with Route 16, is **Wakefield Marketplace**, a farmers' and crafts market open Saturdays, 9:00 A.M. to 4:00 P.M., and other times when produce is plentiful. You'll see the big tent beside the road. If you're heading south, take this turn into the village and continue on the recently designated scenic byway, along country roads shun-piking busy Route 16 from the farmers' market all the way to the New Hampshire Farm Museum in Milton.

Despite all the lakes around, finding a public place to swim can be difficult. **Wentworth Park** on Route 109 between Wakefield and Wolfeboro is a small beach with bathhouses and a picnic area along its sandy shorefront. Nearby is the stone foundation and well of the summer estate of Benning Wentworth, first of New Hampshire's royal governors. This 100-by-40-foot structure with stories 18 feet high and windows 6 feet tall is thought to have been the first summer vacation "cottage" in America, built in 1768. Unfortunately, the estate burned not long after the Revolution. In the summer there is often an archaeological dig here.

Across the street from the beach, there is a small granite marker at the beginning of **Ellie's Woodland Walk at Ryefield Marsh,** one of several walking trails and conservation areas of the Wolfeboro Conservation Commission. Five markers identify important environmental sites along the path, including a birch grove, meadow, beaver marsh, and the animals and plants that inhabit them. This is an easy, flat walk through a lowland area. The trail is open every day, year-round. Close by the granite marker on Route 109 there is a black mailbox where you can pick up a map of the trail and an explanation of the markers.

Another place for swimming in the area is the **Allen A. Albee Town Beach,** also on Lake Wentworth. You'll find the entrance road on the east side of Route 28 (109) just after the **Allen A. Motor Inn.**

For a short but beautiful side trip from Route 28 south of South Wolfeboro, take Robert's Cove Road west. The road will pass by the **Lin-Joy Cabins** (Robert's Cove Road, Alton 03809; 603–569–4973) a set of rustic, summer-camp-style cabins with kitchenettes and a pool. Rates per cabin $50 ($275/week) to $75 ($450). Just beyond the cabins, the road passes between a handsome set of heavily built, new **stone walls** and provides a nice view of an arm of the lake. Guests of the cabins can walk to a small, semiprivate swimming area at the foot of the hill near the marina.

Wolfeboro's Main Street is busy in the summer, but there is a leisurely air here, with no traffic jams.

On the town dock, on the lake side off Main Street in the center of town, *PJ's Dockside* is close to life on the lake. They have a good selection of sandwiches, salads, lobster and clam rolls, and the usual sides of fries. Sandwiches run from $3.50 to $6.00. Seafood dinners run about $11–13. After 5:00 P.M. they have light dinner entrees from $8.00 to $12.00.

The landing for the MV *Judge Sewall* is right out the front door of PJ's. Built in 1946, the boat cruised in the Atlantic before coming to the lake in the late 1980s. Not as big as its better-known rival, its 65-foot hull is big enough to provide a smooth ride, and the enclosed deck and open topside make it pleasant in almost all weather. The narrated cruises take an hour and a half, passing a loon refuge, old boatyards, and several of the lake's islands. For information and reservations, call (603) 569–3016. Board at the Town Dock.

Be sure to walk down Railroad Street and take a look at the restored railroad station where summer visitors once detrained. There's a parking lot here, and just beyond, the *Bridge Falls Walking Trail* follows the former railbed to the Falls section of town. Running 200 yards along the shore of Back Bay, this short and level walk leads to an area that was once used by water-powered mills. After crossing Route 109 (Center Street), the trail continues along the track as far as Sanbornville, but the track and ties have not been removed from a lot of the route, and the going on that side can get difficult.

At the falls, *The Wright Museum* brings memories of World War II to life for those who lived through it and puts flesh on the bones of history for those who don't remember it. The war's effect on the homefront is shown through vehicles, magazines, and even a soda fountain and a dentist's office, while another section exhibits military hardware, including tanks and half tracks. They even have a Norden bombsight, one of the most secret devices of the war. A special section highlights the role of women in the military, including their little-known role as bomber ferry pilots. The museum is at 77 Center Street (Routes 28 and 109) Wolfeboro, (603) 569–1212, and charges a small admission fee.

Close to the Wright museum, is the *"Klickety-Klack" Model Railroad*, a labor-of-love exhibit of model train enthusiast Richard Peasley and friends. There are more than 1000 feet of HO- and N-gauge track, with 22 trains coursing over the track, through the tunnels, and over the bridges. The track passes through realistic villages, over mountains, and through quarry and industrial sites both day and night. You can run eleven of the trains yourself, and signs point out special things in the layout. From Memorial Day to July 1, and from Labor Day through December, it's open Thursday, Friday, and Saturday 10:00 A.M. to 5:00 P.M., from July 1 to Labor Day, Monday–Saturday from 10:00 A.M. to 5:30 P.M. The museum sometimes also opens by appointment, and Richard says its okay to call him at home. A small admission fee is charged. From Route 109, take Route 109A (Elm Street) a few hundred feet; it's on the left. Elm Street, Wolfeboro, (603) 569–5384 or 569–1275 (home).

Wolfeboro has a lot of opportunities for active recreation. If you like fishing, or think that you want to try if in a serious way, consider *Gadabout Golder*, who provides guided fishing trips around Lake Winnipesaukee, in the Pemigewasset, Little Swift, Bear Camp, and Connecticut Rivers. Their trips follow the season and may concentrate on salmon, pike, bass, trout, or any of the many other native species. They take experienced people and amateurs and have fly fishing as well. The full-day rate for two fishing on the lake is about $225 (half-day $175); the rates fluctuate with the destination and species. They also do canoe trips, guided snowshoeing, nature walks, guided tracking trips, and ice fishing on the lake. It's at 79 Middleton Road, Wolfeboro 03894; (603) 569–6426.

The Lakes region also offers lots of bicycling opportunities over terrain that can be hilly or hug the level shorelines. *Nordic Skier Sports* has good, recent model bikes for rent at reasonable prices. They are at 19 North Main Street, Wolfeboro 03894; (603) 569–3151. In winter, they offer 20 kilometers of well-groomed and tracked cross-country trails with lake views. This complete center also has equipment rentals and lessons.

There are a number of choices for hiking and walking in addition to Ellie's. The *Knight's Pond Conservation Area* features a 1.7 mile main trail, with a .3 mile option to the end of a peninsula. Along the way, it passes around the sides of a beaver marsh and a thirty-one-acre pond that has not had any development. From the trail are views of Caverly Mountain, Rines Hill, and Mount Longstack. A trail map and directions are available at the Information Center at the intersection of Main Street and Routes 109 and 28. The center also has a sheet of information on more than a dozen *hiking trails* in the greater Wolfeboro area suitable for family outings.

For kayaking, go to **Winnipesaukee Kayak Company**, which offers rentals and instruction. They have daily and weekly rentals. They are on the west side of Back Bay at 17 Bay Street in Wolfeboro; (603) 569–9926. If you are looking for *canoe and sailboat rentals,* contact **Brewster Academy,** which rents them from their Pinckney Boathouse. They rent by the hour, half and full day, or by the week. Go to the boathouse (on the south end of town, ask anybody) 9:00 A.M. to 4:30 P.M. Monday–Friday or weekends by appointment. Call (603) 569–7136 during hours or 569–4645 after hours. A bit more exotic is **Weirs Parasail,** which operates from Weirs Beach Pier, a quarter mile west of Weirs Beach on Lakeside Drive, off Route 3. For information and reservations, call at (603) 366–7723.

The town also has an active musical arts program that runs from the spring through the fall. The 1997 series included choral works, ragtime, Gilbert and Sullivan, the New England Brass, and much more. There is at least one program a month. For information and reservations, write **Wolfeboro Friends of Music**, P.O. Box 2056, Wolfeboro 03894, (603) 569–3657, 3240 or 3091. Tickets are $8.00–$11.00 with discounts for seniors and students.

If you follow Main Street north along the shore of the lake, you will come to the **Libby Museum** (Route 109, no phone). The focus of the museum is natural history and its exhibits include examples of many of the birds and animals native to the area. There is also a collection of Indian artifacts and items uncovered at excavations at the Wentworth mansion site. In addition to the exhibits, they conduct an Enviro-Arts Summer Program and periodic art exhibits in keeping with the museum's mission. It's open Tuesday through Sundays 10:00 A.M. to 4:00 P.M. during the summer.

The Wolfeboro Historical Society operates the **Clark House Museum Complex,** which includes a replica of a mid-nineteenth-century firehouse, an 1868 school-house, and an eighteenth-century farmhouse. Open Monday through Saturday 10:00 A.M. to 4:00 P.M. in July and August. It's on South Main Street in Wolfeboro; call (603) 569–4997 or 569–3667.

An interesting two-hour cruise of the islands on the east side of Lake Winnipesaukee leaves from Wolfeboro on Saturdays and Sundays at 10:00 A.M., 12:00 noon, and 2:00 P.M. and Friday and Saturday evenings at 6:30 P.M. The captain of the **M/V Doris E** points out interesting features on shore and enlivens the cruise with local stories and history. Light refreshments are available, but if you would like to enjoy a glass of wine with the sunset, you'll have to bring your own. The fare is $8.00 for adults and $4.00 for children. For details call (603) 366–2628.

The **Abenaki Tower,** a little farther along Route 109 in Melvin Village, gives no clue to its origin except the date of its construction. This sturdy wooden structure puts you above the treetops for a 180-degree view over Lake Winnipesaukee and its wooded islands and bays. The Belknap Mountains back it to the south and the Squam Range to the north. It's a short easy walk and then a stiff climb, but the view is spectacular, especially at sunset. Notice the unusual raised lines on the boulder near the trail.

Although there are antiques shops all over the state, some of which come and go within a season or two, there is one in Tuftonboro that is well worth a visit. *Dow's Corner Shop* has occupied its enormous barn for close to fifty years. It is so full of antiques that you have to walk sideways in the narrow aisles. From export china to 1920s fur coats, if you collect it, they'll not only have it, but they will have several to choose from. This is also a good place to find the once popular Kilburn stereoscopic view cards of New Hampshire. Open daily May 1 to October 15 and by chance in the winter. Dow's Corner Shop is on Route 171 at Tuftonboro Corner, R.F.D., Ossipee 03864; (603–539–4790).

Ossipee

Unlike New Hampshire's western border, where the Connecticut River makes a clean separation with Vermont, the border with Maine, north of Wakefield, is merely a surveyor's line. Roads and villages that grew up prior to this line sprawl and meander from one side to the other. Route 153 is one of these, not only a lovely road to travel, but a good alternative for shunpikers seeking to avoid the traffic of Route 16. On its way to Conway, this road weaves through valleys and around the shores of little lakes. Province Lake nudges it over the line into Maine for a few miles until it re-enters New Hampshire at South Effingham.

The Effinghams, and there are four of them, were once a very prosperous community based on a group of mills built along the Ossipee River in the 1820s. Center Effingham overlooks the road from a hill, with an imposing town hall that doubles as a Masonic Lodge. That accounts for the emblem on the clock face. A grange hall, a church, and several homes complete the historic village.

To the north is Effingham, also known as Lord's Hill. This cluster of early nineteenth-century buildings includes a church, a 1780s hip-roofed house, and several impressive homes of 1820s origin. Just down from the crest of the hill is a road with a historic marker describing the Effingham Union Academy, New Hampshire's first state teachers college. A short distance up that road, set among manicured lawns and huge shade trees, is *Squire Lord's mansion.* For its size and the quality of its architecture, this would be an impressive building in Portsmouth or Exeter. Here, come upon suddenly in such a rural setting, it is astonishing. Its three stories rise in clean lines, the eye drawn upward to the tall, octagonal, domed cupola. A Palladian window in the second floor surmounts the wide Federal doorway. No longer open for public tours, the mansion is now a private home. Please respect this and continue down the road a few yards to the academy to turn around.

The town of Freedom lies along a small river, its two streets lined by fine homes, many with interesting decorative trim. On Maple Street is the *Freedom Historical Society,* whose collections include furnished rooms. The Victorian parlor is particularly illustrative of life in these prosperous mill towns during their heyday, with its ornate fainting couch and stereoscope viewer. Open Tuesday, Thursday, Saturday, and Sunday, 2:00 to 4:00 P.M.

If you're staying at **Purity Spring Resort,** you don't have to look for activities to keep your family busy, since each day at this casual family resort brings new activities, from a Monday morning breakfast cooked over a campfire and Thursday lobster and steak cookout on their private island to the Friday night steamship smorgasbord. The dining room in the old-fashioned American-plan resort offers a choice of five entrees each evening, always including a meatless alternative. Non-guests are welcome at meals—some families come every week for the lobster cookout.

Everything here is included: day care, tennis, canoes, rowboats, and all outdoor activities, except an all-day canoe trip on the nearby Saco River. Grandparents who first came here as children are still returning to this comfortable, homey resort. It is also handicapped accessible. Write them at East Madison 03849; telephone (800) 367–8897 from the United States or Canada.

King Pine Ski Area just up the road is small, but it has trails for those of all skill levels. Six trails and slopes are lighted for night skiing. Facilities are up to date, but prices are old-fashioned and made even better with joint ski-lodging packages with Purity Spring. A complete ski school and the relaxed atmosphere of King Pine make it a particular favorite of families. It's located on Route 153 in East Madison; call (800) 367–8897.

The **Madison Boulder,** off Route 113 between Conway and Madison, is the largest known example of a glacial erratic in New England, and one of the largest in the world. Enormous freestanding boulders are not uncommon in New Hampshire, but none even approaches the size of this 83-foot, 5,000-ton giant.

This is not just another big rock. Such erratics were broken from large outcrops of granite by glaciers, then carried away and dropped in spots sometimes several miles distant. This one is thought to have come from cliffs about 4 miles away, but some geologists believe that it came from Mount Willard, 25 miles north in Crawford Notch.

On the side of a steep hill overlooking a panorama of mountains, **Snow Village Inn** has a knockout location. Rooms are in the main building, a country retreat built in 1900 by the historian Frank Simonds, and in two nicely adapted adjacent buildings, one of which has fireplaces in each room. The best view is from the second-floor Robert Frost room, where you wake up facing a vista that spans from Mt. Chocorua to Maine, including Mt. Washington. It's a long way to a restaurant, so the new owners have created a menu to match the views, with such entrees as roast duck or grilled shrimp with roasted red-pepper puree. The four-course dinner is included, along with a full breakfast, in the $129–$219 per couple rate. Those who are not staying at the Inn are welcome to the dining room with prior reservations and can order entrees that range from $16 to $24. Special events include snowshoeing (the inn provides the snowshoes), cooking, and wine weekends. The previous owners of this well-loved inn are a hard act to follow, but the Flynns are hearing rousing applause for their own show. For reservations write them at Snowville 03849 or call (603) 447–2818 or (800) 447–4345.

You can arrive at the Snow Village by bicycle (we'd walk them up the last steep hill to the inn) in a **Bike the**

Whites package that includes a night here, one at the *Tamworth Inn,* and one at *The Forest Inn* (see page 186). Beginning on Sundays, the tours include breakfasts and dinners, maps with points of interest noted, luggage transfers, transportation to the starting point, and emergency assistance if needed en route. For information, write The Tamworth Inn, Box 189, Tamworth 03886 or call (800) 933–3902.

Overlooking the postcard-perfect Crystal Lake in "downtown" Eaton, *The Inn at Crystal Lake* looks exactly like what it is—a hostelry that has welcomed travelers to this tiny village since the 1880s. Its three layers of porches, rows of rockers, and columned façade mark it even before you see the sign. Inside this period piece, simply furnished rooms are comfortable and breakfasts delicious. It no longer has a full dining room, but guests have the happy option of making a dinner reservation at the nearby Snow Village Inn. Route 153, Eaton Center 03832; (603) 447–2120 or (800) 343–7336.

White Lake State Park packs three attractions into one compact park that surrounds a crystal-clear lake. The lake's swimming beach stretches along one end, with the rest of the shore bordered in trees. A walking trail encircles its perimeter, and a campground offers well-spaced sites under tall pine trees, the forest floor padded by a soft carpet of pine needles. Across the lake is a stand of *pitch pines* that have been declared a National Natural Landmark. Close to the northern tip of their range, the pitch pines here are especially large, which indicates age, but they are hard to date because they don't grow even rings for each year's growth. Pitch pine trees have difficulty reproducing except after a forest fire, since their cones need the heat to spring them open and release the seeds. Open from the end of May to Columbus Day, White Lake is in Tamworth; call (603) 323–7350.

Another interesting pine-forest environment is located a short distance away along the road between Silver Lake and West Ossipee. The **West Branch Pine Barrens,** part of which is owned by the Nature Conservancy, is considered one of the world's finest examples of pine barrens. Its layer of birch and scrub oak grows under a canopy of pitch pine, with blueberry bushes closer to the ground. The barrens is home to several rare moth varieties that feed on its trees.

Just north of the village of Chocorua, you'll see a sign for the **Riverbend Country Inn** on the west side of Route 16. Although only a short distance from the traffic, it seems to be deep in the woods. The inn overlooks a deep curve in the Chocorua River, and in good weather guests have breakfast outside on a terrace that extends out over the riverbank. The inn is as lovely as its setting, with bright airy guest rooms and antiques-furnished public rooms. Little details, such as a kitchenette where tea and cookies are always available, make guests feel pampered. Write to the inn at P.O. Box 347, Chocorua 03817; call (603) 323–7440 or (800) 628–6944.

Don't be put off by the fear of looking like the two fat pink pigs on the sign of **The Yankee Smokehouse** at the intersection of Routes 16 and 25 in West Ossipee. This is an authentic open-pit barbecue, one of the few in New England. The service is so unremittingly cheerful and

They're Smaller Now

The snowmobile was invented by Virgil White, longtime owner of White's Garage, a familiar landmark in West Ossipee, where more than 20,000 of these were made between 1913 and 1929. They worked on two axles of rear wheels joined by caterpillar traction, fitted onto a Ford chassis with two runners on the front; he patented the name, along with the machine.

eager here that it reminds us of Disney World. Servers describe each specialty and suggest the best deal. "You'll get more of the same thing for less money by ordering the sampler for one and splitting it," our waiter once advised us after mentally totting up our order. Beef or pork ribs or slices, chicken, and delicious baby back pork ribs are their specialties, but you can have the sliced smoked beef or pork in a sandwich or the chicken made into a wonderful smoked salad. Don't miss the corn chowder (it's unlikely that your waiter will allow you to order a meal without it), which is solid with chunks of potato, bacon, and corn, seasoned with herbs and plenty of pepper. You can roll up your sleeves and eat until you can't hold another bite here and have trouble making the bill come out to $10 each. If you have a group of at least eight, order the Smokehouse Feast for $47.95. It says on the menu that it feeds four to six, but it's enough for a regiment on the march. Open all year, except April and from mid-November to mid-December (telephone 603–539–RIBS).

South of the Yankee Smokehouse on Route 16, a former state fish hatchery has been converted to ***Sumner Brook***

Fish Farm. Fly-fishing enthusiasts can practice their skills in the pond on a catch-and-release basis, or those who prefer can catch their supper at 30 cents an inch. The farm also sells trout or will stock your own pond. Open weekends spring and fall, daily Memorial Day through Labor Day (603) 539–7232.

The Sandwiches

Some of New Hampshire's quirky private museums—collections gathered over the years by people with a particular hobby or interest—have signs by the roadside inviting people in, and some don't. Even when you're in *The Old Country Store,* at the crossroads in Moultonboro, you might not notice the sign by the stairs pointing to the museum. The whole upper floor is filled with local history—saws, axes, and other tools; a wooden snow shovel; blacksmithing tools; maple sugaring equipment; advertising cards; cigar store Indians; yarn winders—neatly labeled, often in some detail. There is no curator and no charge; you just wander around at your leisure. You might want to show your appreciation by taking home some common crackers or some cheddar cheese from the wheel in the glass case downstairs or stopping for a Moxie or a cream soda from the big old ice chest, but everybody's very pleasant even if you don't buy anything. Outside in the barn is an original Concord Coach that is thought to be the oldest Concord-built stagecoach in existence.

The Village of Center Sandwich is largely made up of houses built in the first half of the nineteenth century. The houses are clustered into a handful of tree-lined streets, an open invitation to stroll through town. Along with the antiques and craft shops, be sure to stop at the **Sandwich Historical Society Museum.** Its furnishings include a kitchen, household implements, and a wide variety of artifacts from the town's eighteenth-century beginnings through the early twentieth century. Open, free of charge, Monday through Saturday, 11:00 A.M. to 5:00 P.M. in July and August and 1:00 to 5:00 P.M. June and September (603–284–6665).

Follow Grove Street and then bear left at road signs for **Sandwich Notch**. It is reached by a gravel road that is not maintained for winter use. The stone walls beside it once outlined the fields of farms, now overgrown into forests. A cart track, the road was put through the notch in 1801 as a route for north-country farmers to get their produce to the markets of Portsmouth and Portland and return with supplies and goods not produced on their own farms. Later bypassed by other routes, the road through this notch has not changed very much for the past century-and-a-half.

A parking area on the right marks the short trail to **Beede's Falls.** Where the trail meets the river, an island cuts the river into two small channels. To the right, the water slides over ledges and drops in a series of cascades into a moss-lined pool below. The wooded area at the bottom is surrounded by a tumble of boulders, some of which form caves and crevices. If you go upstream along the island, you will see the brook rushing through a foot-wide shoot. A short distance above that, the river flows down a ledge and then drops 40 feet into a sandy pool. More rocks lie in giant tumbles here, too. Some of these overhang enough to form a cave

T H

want peace,
and space for
them for rates
ion. Rockywold-
ess 03245; (603)

ire on Route 113 in
explore six different
ibit trail. Signs and
stems of the marsh,
e, showing how plants
ch setting. Signboards
e marsh were drained,
community is reached by
ith little bodies lying on
nted turtles, leopard frogs,
e everywhere, perched on
ng among trees. The setting
aintained, a good way to
elds, and waters as you travel
ng travelers will enjoy the
er, where they can descend into
b a giant spiderweb, or invent an
sign.

ns at the Center are the Nature
ake on their own 28-foot pontoon
and *Merganser.* There are several
eaving before 6:00 A.M. and as late as
rent days of the week, so it's best to
for the schedule. Cruise fees are $12
depart from the Science Center. There is
ng new songbird exhibit and aviary.

Get Your Big Foot out of My Sandwich

*H*ollis is not alone as a siting spot for Sasquatch. In the area around Sandwich—Mount Israel and Sandwich Dome—have been reports since the early 1940s, and they have even been backed up by 3-foot-long footprints, four-toed and clawless, like other Big Foot tracks recorded, in the mud beside the road. Recent reports on file with the State Police all describe a fur-covered creature about 8 feet tall. Everyone agrees that however startled and alarmed they were, Big Foot seemed just as frightened, and ran into the woods immediately.

that, legend has it, sheltered a stray cow for an entire winter. Above the main falls there are two more cascades. Because there are no signs here, it would be easy to miss the main falls to the left and to assume the cascades downstream to be Beede's Falls.

Not far up the road, between two bridges over the Bearcamp River, is a cliff shaped like the prow of a ship. Called **Pulpit Rock,** it was used as a pulpit by a long-ago Quaker pastor. The head of the notch, 7 miles from the center of Center Sandwich Village, is marked by a small sign high up on a tree and not easy to see. For a well-written history of the notch, read *The Road Through Sandwich Notch* by Elizabeth Yates.

There are more entrees on the daily special blackboard at **The Corner House** in Center Sandwich than most restaurants have on their printed menu. These dishes allow the chef to take advantage of ingredients with short seasons and the chance to serve his latest original dish. This might be a double lamb chop stuffed with a blend of ricotta, parmesan, and spinach. The printed menu is not ho-hum either, with such offerings as medallions of chicken breast stuffed with ham and artichoke hearts or veal smothered in chunks of lo⊦ with broccoli and béarnaise sauce. A gri⌐ nutmeg on the cappuccino tops off a fine Prices are moderate; lunch (try the crabcake⌐ every day except Sunday in the summer Wednesday through Saturday in the winter. D⌐ served every summer evening from 5:30 P.M. Wednesday through Sunday in the winter.

Upstairs there are four moderately priced guest room⌐ decorated with a stylish Victorian flair. Furnishings include brass and oak beds, wicker chairs, hand-hooked rugs, spool towel racks, marble-topped bureaus, and prints that range from Godey's *Lady's Book* illustrations to French impressionist exhibition posters. Open year-round; write The Corner House, Box 204, Center Sandwich 03227 or call (603) 284–6219.

Squam

T he quiet of Squam Lake is almost legendary. Its irregular shape, with bays, inlets, and islands, makes it virtually impossible for power boats to get up any speed, so there is very little to disturb the loons that nest there. Cottages along the shore are tucked behind the trees, giving it the feel of a wilderness lake.

Squam, along with Winnipesaukee, is one of the best landlocked salmon lakes in the state. If you want to try your luck, call Captain Joe Nassar, a licensed *fishing guide*. His rate for one to three people for four hours is

even think about this place. If you camaraderie, connection with nature, thought, you'll find it here. Call or writ⌐ and family packages; it's all by reserva⌐ Deephaven Camps, P.O. Box B, Holder⌐ 968–3313.

The *Science Center of New Hamps⌐* Holderness encourages visitors to⌐ natural communities along its ec⌐ staff members explain the eco⌐ field, pond, stream, forest, and la⌐ and animals live together in e⌐ explore such questions as "If⌐ who would suffer?" The marsh⌐ a boardwalk, often covered⌐ their stomachs watching pa⌐ and trout below. Birds a⌐ fences or signposts or dar⌐ is attractive and well⌐ understand the woods,⌐ around the state. Yo⌐ Children's Activity Cen⌐ a groundhog hole, clim⌐ insect of their own de⌐

The newest attracti⌐ Cruises on Squam⌐ boats, the *Heron⌐* different cruises,⌐ 7:00 P.M. on diff⌐ check with the⌐ per person and⌐ also an excit⌐

fi⌐ ou⌐ Mea⌐ dining stored in cabin dai⌐ lodges also s⌐ fashioned fam⌐ thought had le⌐ conveniences, cre⌐

Admission during July an~
and $3.00 for children. In M~
October the rate drops by half. S~
9:30 A.M. to 4:00 P.M.; spring and fa~
on weekdays but 1:00 to 4:00 P.M.~
Sundays. For a calendar of the Science
special events write P.O. Box 173, Holdernes~
(603) 968–7194.

In 1904, the heir of the man who invented
manufactured the soda fountain built a brick summ~
home in Center Harbor overlooking Squam Lake and
the Squam mountain range. Unlike many northern
homes, it had wide hallways, huge windows, and other
elements of southern architecture; it was a showplace,
even in an area rich in opulent private estates. It passed
from his family through several owners, including
minor European royalty, and eventually became
Belknap College, which failed in the mid-1970s.

In 1985 its present owners bought the property and
immediately began to restore and refurnish it to its
original style. The result is **Red Hill Inn,** a period-piece
mansion that visitors would gladly pay admission to
tour. The inn is both lodging and restaurant, and it does
both equally well. Despite its Victorian air, the relaxed
feeling of a vacation home is still strong. Guest rooms
and suites are bright and airy, with spectacular views
over lawns, gardens, and the estate's farmhouse and
barns to Squam Lake and the mountains beyond. In the
evenings from the front rooms, dining room, and
terrace, you can watch the setting sun turn the sky and
lake to gold, the lawn to a brighter green, and the facing
mountainsides dark with long shadows.

attention, even with the
...ı with half of a giant Spanish
...oke hearts and aged cheddar.
...rk tender, is in a caper sauce with
...es, and young tender rabbit is served
...rown sauce. Desserts change daily and
...riginal: apricot pie, Kentucky High (with
...and chocolate), and two old-time Yankee
...ies—Indian pudding and vinegar pie. That's
...you won't have a chance to try anywhere else.
...appuccino and espresso are offered, along with a nice
selection of teas. Prices are moderate.

The bar in the lounge is half of a wooden hulled Chris-Craft one of the owners bought after an accident had ruined the other side. The entire inn is decorated with the owners' collections, including several groups of early cameras. In the summer, guests can hike to tiny secluded beaches on Squam's shores, where the bottom is sandy and the water shallow enough for children to splash in safety for quite a distance. Rates for rooms and suites in the inn and the adjacent farmhouse vary with size and location, from $75 to $145 including a country breakfast. Write Red Hill Inn, Box 99M, Center Harbor 03226; call (603) 279–7001 or (800) 5–REDHILL.

Winter visitors to the Squam area can enjoy cross-country skiing free of charge at the **Red Hill Ski Touring Center** on Route 25B in Center Harbor. Intermediate- and beginner-level trails lead along the hillside meadows, through the woods, and along the shores of the lake. Rental ski equipment is available at Red Hill Inn.

PLACES TO STAY
IN THE LAKES AND FOOTHILLS
(ALL AREA CODES 603)

WOLFEBORO
Tuc-Me-Inn Bed and Breakfast,
118 North Main Street, 03894;
569–5702. Comfortable, 7 rooms,
3 with private bath, 4 share two
bathrooms. Double $75–$85, $10
less off-season, including full
breakfast.

ALTON BAY
Lakehurst Housekeeping
Cottages, Route 11–D, 03810;
875–2492. Available May and
June by the night; July, August,
and September by the week only.
Nice, well-kept cottages on the
water. Reservations suggested,
heavily booked. One bedroom
$65/night, $450/week; two
bedroom $75/night, $550/week.

FREEDOM
Freedom House Bed and
Breakfast, Maple Street, 03836;
539–4815. A beautifully restored
Victorian home in the center of
the village, open year-round.

MADISON
Maple Grove House, Maple Grove
Road, 367–8208. Large rooms in
a renovated Victorian
farmhouse.

Col.
baths, .

MOULTONBO
Olde Orchard
Road, 03254; 476
598–5845. A 1700s f.
home; doubles from $7

TAMWORTH
The Tamworth Inn, Cleveland
Hill Road, 03886; (800)
NH2–RELAX. A nicely restored
village inn a few steps from the
Barnstormers' summer
playhouse. Rooms and suites, all
with private bath at $95 to $145;
the dining room is among the
best in the area.

Whispering Pines Bed &
Breakfast, Route 113A at
Hemenway Road, 03886;
323–7337. A location doesn't get
much quieter than this; some
rooms have private baths.
Moderate rates, full breakfast.

ASHLAND
Little Holland Court, Route 3,
968–4434. Housekeeping
cottages $60–$135 per night,
$350–$750 per week.

HOLDERNESS
The Inn on Golden Pond, Route
3, P.O. Box 680, 03245; 968–7269.
Beautiful Inn/B&B

..ILFORD
Victorian House, 2645 Lakeshore
Drive, 03246; 293–8155.
Wonderful appetizers and nice
entrees: steak, duck, veal and
lobster. Victorian setting on
pleasant grounds. Entrees
$15–$22, most at $18.

WEST OSSIPEE
Whittier House Restaurant,
Route 16, 539–4513. A bright
and airy dining room serving
lunch and dinner daily at
moderate prices.

Both Purity Spring Resort and
Snow Village Inn, in the
preceding text, have dining
rooms open to the public.

MOULTONBOROUGH
Sweetwater Inn, Route 25,
476–5079. An innovative Italian
menu, with excellent veal dishes
and moderate prices.

The Woodshed, Lee's Mill Road,
476–2311. Best known for its
prime rib and lamb, and for its
breads; moderate prices.

ASHLAND
The Common Man, Route 3,
968–7030. Right in the center of
town, with a dependable and
varied lunch and dinner menu;
moderate prices.

For other dining options, see
Plymouth, page 137.

...e 3,
..ming
..erlooking
..uble $85–$95,
..armet breakfast.

..sed Petals Inn, Shepard
..oad, 03245; 968–4417,
..utside New Hampshire (800)
839–6205. Elegant country inn
in the Victorian style. Double
$99–$118, including full
breakfast and afternoon tea.

PLACES TO EAT
IN THE LAKES AND FOOTHILLS
(ALL AREA CODES 603)

WOLFEBORO
Mast Landing, Main Street,
03894; 569–1789. Classic town
diner, breakfast and lunch daily.
Inexpensive.

Bittersweet, Route 28, 03896;
569–3636. North and east of
Wolfeboro. European and
American, in rustic barn
setting. May to December,
dinners Monday–Saturday and
Sunday brunch from 11:00 A.M.
to 2:00 P.M.

The Eastern White Mountains

The White Mountains are the stuff of Indian legend and settlers' folk tales, of larger-than-life explorers and pioneers. Until the discovery of Crawford Notch, these mountains presented a barrier that kept the lands to the north in isolation.

In the nineteenth century they were "discovered" again, this time by wealthy families from the cities escaping the heat and dust. With maids, nannies, and enormous trunks, entire families boarded trains in New York, New Haven, Boston, Hartford, and other cities bound for Jackson, Glen, Twin Mountain, and Bretton Woods. Hotels sent elegant Concord Coaches, resplendent in canary yellow or cherry red with gold-leaf scrollwork, to welcome guests. They stayed all summer, hiking, riding, swimming (called "bathing"), playing lawn sports, and dancing to a full orchestra every evening. This annual social season lasted until World War II and the invention of air conditioning. Now most of the grand hotels are gone, but the few that remain have retained the fine traditions that made them famous in their golden age.

The Eastern White Mountains

Twin Mtn.

Mount Washington +

3

Crawford Notch

MOUNT WASHINGTON

Mt. Lafayette +

302

Pinham Notch

WILDCAT VALLEY

16

Jackson

MAINE

NEW HAMPSHIRE

North Conway

112

KANCAMAGUS

KANKAMAGUS HWY.

Conway

16

Waterville Valley

WATERVILLE VALLEY

49

93

N

0   10 mi
0   10 km

THE EASTERN WHITE MOUNTAINS' TOP PICKS

The Cascades

Welch-Dickey Mountain Trail

Sabbaday Falls

Rail 'n River Forest Trail

Indian Museum

Diana's Baths

Conway Scenic Railway

North Conway Depot

Mt. Washington Observatory Resource Center

Abenaki Encampment and Shop

Wentworth Resort

Jackson Falls

Jackson Ski Touring Foundation

The Inn at Thorn Hill

Heritage New Hampshire

Glen Ellis Falls

Lost Pond

Crystal Cascade

Livermore

Mount Willard

Jefferson Notch

Cog Railway Museum

Mount Washington Hotel

Zealand Falls

Waterville Valley

Waterville Valley is a cul-de-sac cut deep into the White Mountain National Forest. Route 49 follows the Mad River, which is really quite benign except in the spring when it carries the runoff from a vast watershed and pours it into the Pemigewasset River. After 12 miles of narrow wooded passage, the valley opens suddenly into a broad floor of fields and a resort village reminiscent of an Alpine ski town.

Best known for its ski area, with the most ski terrain and lifts of any in New Hampshire, Waterville is also a favorite of families who feel perfectly safe letting their children travel between slopes and lodging in this isolated and hometown atmosphere. Its children's ski school has an area all of its own and is considered one of the nation's best places for children to learn to ski. Although Waterville has the atmosphere of a small resort, its facilities are state of the art and waits for lifts up Mount Tecumseh are rare indeed. Cross-country trails, sleigh rides through the White Mountain–ringed landscape, and an indoor skating rink complete the winter activities.

Waterville also includes 22 miles of hiking trails and several mountain summits whose trails begin in the valley. One of the shorter trails for more casual hiking begins at the bottom of the Snow's Mountain ski lift and leads to *The Cascades.* Follow the signs, climbing up the ski slope and then to the left. Be sure that you are following the sign for the Cascades trail and *not* the Snow's Mountain cross-country ski trail. Once you are in the woods, look for yellow trail blazes. There are very few steep places on this easy trail. Once you get to the cascades, cross the brook and continue up the other side for the best views of the continuous series of waterfalls and pools.

A pleasant, if moderately difficult hike, **The Welch-Dickey Mountain Trail** combines views and natural history with a touch of mystery. To reach the trailhead parking area, take Upper Mad River Road, near the Thornton town line, then follow signs at the third junction to the right. Two trails begin here, joined into a loop that connects the two small mountains; the easier route begins with the right-hand trail toward Welch Mountain. Much of the trail is in the open, across ledges that give good views to the south and east. Before reaching the summit of Welch Mountain, the trail passes several stands of jack pine, exceedingly rare in New Hampshire. On Dickey Mountain, look for a cairn marking a stone circle carved into the bedrock. The origin of the circle is unknown, but if you stand inside it and look back toward the large triangular rock, you are looking at the exact point of the sunrise at the summer solstice. The 4½-mile climb takes about three-and-a-half hours.

Okay, we admit it: We like the trappings of luxury, and our favorite place to stay in the valley is *The Snowy Owl.* Summer or winter, its three-story-tall fieldstone fireplace identifies it as a ski lodge. In the big downstairs lounge area, a sunken pit provides guests a place to gather by the fire in the evening. In the afternoon, wine and cheese await returning hikers and skiers. Rooms are spacious; especially nice are the upper-level rooms with loft bunks for the kids. In-suite whirlpool baths, an indoor swimming pool, and a kids-stay-free policy make this contemporary inn an old-fashioned value.

For a cozy dinner and about as close to Switzerland as you'll get in New Hampshire, dine at *The William Tell*, on the Waterville access road, Route 49, in Thornton. The menu is Swiss and continental, preparation exacting, and the decor is authentic, stopping well short of the cutsey-alpiney look. Their *roesti* are as good as any at Zermatt. It's open daily in the winter, closed Wednesdays the rest of the year. Prices are moderate. It's popular on weekends, so you'll want to call (603) 726–3618 for reservations.

For a really off-the-beaten-path dinner—you can't drive there—take a ride on the grooming machine on a winter evening to *Schwendi Hutte*, at the top of a 4,000-foot mountain for a five-course dinner. Saturday nights only, late December through March, and by prior reservation. Pricey, but an experience you'll remember; call (603) 236–8311.

Except in winter, when the road is closed, a nice alternative route out of the valley is over *Thornton Gap*, a small notch reached from a road to the left at the village library. Follow signs to Tripoli (pronounced "triple-eye") Road, following a mountain brook through the forest.

After you crest the gap, you drop down into the Pemigewasset valley near *Russell Pond Campground.* For those who enjoy camping as a sport, not simply as a way to reduce lodging costs, this National Forest campground offers well-separated sites, deep in a hardwood forest that drops into a lovely small pond. No buildings mar its shore; there are a canoe launch, a fisherman or two, and the deep quiet that only lakes that ban motor boats can offer. There are no showers at the campground and no RV hookups. It's hard to believe that such quiet wilderness can be so close to an interstate highway.

The Kancamagus

Only one road cuts directly east and west through the center section of the White Mountain National Forest—the Kancamagus Highway. Not really a highway, but a paved two-lane road, it climbs from Lincoln to Conway over the 2,860-foot Kancamagus

OFF THE BEATEN PATH

Authors' Note

Y*ou should be aware that the White Mountain National Forest has the dubious distinction of being chosen for a pilot program of charging for the use of the national forests. A $20 charge ($5.00 for a one-week pass) is levied not on the person, but on the car, whether you take a five-minute walk to a waterfall or spend the whole summer hiking. You can use the trails all you want as long as somebody drops you off or you park outside the national forest. As we write, little green cars are patrolling like hawks (but are not "authorized" to sell you the passes—you have to go to Lincoln, Conway, or Pinkham Notch to buy them!). Since it's a pilot, no one knows exactly how it will work in the long run, but you should ask at information booths or call (603) 528–8721 for the current status of the plan. Canada has done this with their national parks for years, and it's happening in other states as well. Don't blame New Hampshire, as many people have done quite loudly: It was a decision made in Washington, NOT, we can assure you, something the state volunteered for.*

On the plus side, the Forest Service and the White Mountain Interpretive Association provide free nature programs all summer long at the campgrounds throughout the national forest. You may learn about medicinal plants, weather, lumbering, raptors, canoeing, animals, llama trekking, salmon, geology, or any other facet of the White Mountains. Programs begin at 7:30 P.M. on Friday and Saturday evenings at Dolly Copp Campground, Saturday nights in others. For a schedule, stop at any Ranger Station or call (603) 466–2713.

Pass via a long switchback. Be sure to stop at the pull-out areas to enjoy the view back across the mountains. No commercial development mars this route; you'll just find the woods, the views, small trailhead parking areas, and a handful of National Forest campgrounds.

176

At its beginning is **Loon Mountain**, well known for its ski area. Less known is the geological site at its summit, reached by a trail from the top of its chairlift (which runs in the summer). A well-built stairway allows you to climb down among a tumble of giant boulders tossed there by the glacier to form caves and passageways that will fascinate kids (and adults). If you're there with kids, be sure to take them to meet the Mountain Man, a "hermit" who will show them his cabin and talk about living off—and with—the land, as early settlers did. It borders on hokey but is saved by the skill of the actor, who never makes up something just to answer a question, so what your kids hear is good information to help them understand not only how this land was settled but the interrelationship between humans and nature. An herb woman talks about wild plants in another cabin—all for the cost of the gondola ride. On Sunday mornings, there is a nondenominational service in an outdoor chapel at the summit.

At valley level, the **Wildlife Theater** presents lively shows with native animals, birds, and reptiles, very informative and very popular with kids, who jump at the chance to actually pet a snake and love watching the ferret "weasel its way" through a PVC pipe. Again, the emphasis is on learning about the environment. The park also has an Equestrian Center. It is located on the Kancamagus Highway; call (603) 745–8111.

At the eastern end, watch the south side of the road for the sign for **Sabbaday Falls.** From the picnic area, the path is broad, smooth, and quite well marked to the foot of a flume, where the river flows through a 10-foot gap between straight rock walls more than 40 feet high. At the base there is a water-worn pothole about 4 feet in diameter, and nearby a 2-foot-wide stripe of dark basalt runs through the granite shelf that forms the viewing platform.

The trail along the rim is secured by a log railing, so you can safely look straight down into the flume. Full-grown trees cling to the opposite wall, their roots like giant fingers gripping the rock. You can see here very clearly the dramatic upstream march of the vertical wall of a waterfall. As potholes are formed by whirlpools, their walls are washed or worn away and the ledges are undercut.

About 3 miles east of the Sabbaday Falls trailhead is the Russell-Colbath house. This 1805 farmhouse has been restored to the mid-nineteenth century, providing an interesting look at the isolated lives of the families who settled the Passaconaway Valley. The house is open daily 9:00 A.M. to 4:30 P.M. between mid-June and Labor Day and on weekends after Memorial Day and until Columbus Day.

Behind the house, **Rail 'n River Forest Trail** is a half-mile, level loop that offers a unique view of the logging that once took place here and of the regrowth of the forest. Signboards and a free leaflet explain different kinds of forest environments, how timber was carried out of the valley by rail, and methods used to fight forest fires. The tale of the timbering that once stripped this entire area of its forests is now told only by ghosts, such as the pilings of a railroad bridge in the bed of the Swift River, visible from this trail. For a closer look at these rough-and-tumble days read *Tall Trees, Tough Men* by Robert E. Pike. The trail is wheelchair accessible.

Before the town of Conway and busy Route 16 you will reach Baldy's. This single building houses a small grocery store, a snowshoe shop, and an *Indian Museum.* The last two are the reason for our stop. Treffle Bolduc (Baldy) lived with the northern tribes and learned snowshoe making from them. You'll find his snowshoes all over northern New Hampshire, not only because they last, but because his prices are so reasonable that you can afford to outfit the whole family with snowshoes. Indian lore has been a lifetime interest for Baldy, and his collection of artifacts includes stone projectiles, baskets, cornhusk masks, snowshoes, quill baskets, birchbark containers, beaded mukluks, soapstone carving, and a birchbark canoe. This is not a fancy museum, but rather a collector's treasure trove, displayed in two small rooms with about as much light as the inside of a tepee. But it's real and reflects one man's zeal to preserve and treasure a way of life that very few people have shared. Admission is $5.00 for adults, $2.00 for children; the museum is open daily from 2:00 to 5:00 P.M., except in the winter, when it closes at 4:00 P.M. The store is open longer hours, into the evening in the summer, so someone will probably let you into the museum at times other than its official hours. Call (603) 447–5287 for information.

On Route 16, after it becomes the main street of Conway, you'll see the *Eastman Lord House*, a museum run by the local historical society. It's no ordinary period house, but an 1818 home with each of its twelve rooms restored to a different period, from the year of its building to 1945. The last is the kitchen. Instead of showcases of artifacts with placards, each item is displayed in its place of use, so it's like walking from era to era through someone's home. Their enlightened view of history as a continuing story has created a museum well worth seeing. It's open Memorial Day through Labor Day, Tuesday and Thursday 6:00 to 8:00 P.M., Wednesday 2:00 to 4:00 P.M., and by appointment other days in the summer, and May and September.

Route 16 from the northern end of Conway to above North Conway is so beaten a path that on summer and fall weekends the traffic may be backed up for hours. But there is a way around it, and it takes you past two delightful corners that people honking their horns on Route 16 never hear about. But first you have to find West Side Road. Just opposite the intersection where Route 153 heads south to Eaton Center is a street going north. Take it and then the left at the fork (straight ahead is one of Conway's **covered bridges,** and to the left you will pass another one just a few yards up the road). Follow this road through lovely farmlands that open out to some of the valley's finest views of the Presidential Range.

When the road comes to a T, you should go left to bypass North Conway, or right to reach the ski area or the northern edge, above the outlets.

Less than a mile to the north, on the left of West Side Road, is the unmarked trailhead to **Diana's Baths.** Look for a wide, straight, gravel road, between two fenced fields, which ends abruptly at the edge of the woods. Only here will you finally find the signs identifying the trail.

The falls, only ½ mile along a fairly level trail, were once the site of a gristmill. You can still see the foundations and the chute that fed it water. Above, falls and pools are interspersed with cascades over sloping granite. Each of these succeeding shelves is marked by potholes cut into its surface, like a series of children's marble holes on a playground. As you continue to climb, you will find the ledges flatten and the falls shorten. But the swirls and scoops in the granite become even more dramatic.

Another way of getting to North Conway without encountering the outlet traffic, is to ride the **Conway Scenic Railway** from the quieter town of Conway. The tracks cut through the peaceful, historic heart of the valley, passing fields, meadows, woodlands, the Saco River, and an abandoned lumber mill. The Presidential Range fills the north end of the valley and dramatic ledges line the west. Or, if you begin the trip in North Conway, you can enjoy a good lunch en route in the dining car, a period piece in honey-colored wood and etched glass. Trains run daily from mid-May through foliage season, weekends as early as April and as late as September, but in order to ride from Conway and have any time in North Conway, you have to ride between May and October when there are multiple trains each day. The train also travels north to Bartlett and, once a day, beyond, and all the way through Crawford Notch to the tiny Victorian railway station that once served Crawford House. It's five hours of mountain scenery and a don't-look-down crossing of the Frankenstein Trestle. The trains begin at the depot in downtown North Conway; call (603) 356–5251 or (800) 232–5251.

You don't have to ride the train to enjoy the museum at the **North Conway Depot,** a beautifully restored Victorian railway station in the center of town at the northern terminus of the trip. Displayed in the old waiting room are brochures, lanterns, uniforms, photos, and other historical items. Be sure to ask for the flyer identifying the buildings, railway cars, and engines in the rail yard. Many of the cabooses are private homes; other cars and engines are in the process of restoration. Telephone (603) 356–5251.

Before the return ride to Conway, walk across the wide town green to *Zebs General Store,* which carries only products made in New England. Look for fine foods from small farms and bakeries, unique handmade items, books, soaps, and an array of other items you won't find elsewhere.

Just south of North Conway, US 302 diverges east from Route 16 through a dot on the map marked Redstone. This was once a very active village because of the Redstone Ledge, where a richly colored red granite was quarried, and because of a spring known for its restorative properties. During the Victorian era, "taking the cure" became high fashion, and grand hotels were built around springs whose water tasted even faintly odd. These mineral springs were fairly common in Vermont and the Hudson Valley, but quite uncommon in New Hampshire, where we've been able to track only three. All that's left of the fashionable *White Mountain Mineral Springs* is some foundation stones and one of the most surprising sights you'll come upon in a walk through the New Hampshire woods.

Only a short distance from the Route 16 intersection, look for a pull-out area in a pine forest, where you'll see a gate barring an old road. You'll also see a sign and a trail map, but you won't need a map. Park and follow the

Bit of a Blow, It Was

On April 12, 1934, the highest velocity wind gust ever recorded rocked the Observatory on top of Mount Washington with a force of 231 miles per hour. On the same day, the one-hour average velocity was as high 173 miles per hour, also a record.

old road on foot through woods and across a power-line cut to a large, round field. As you enter the field, look to the woods on your right. You'll see what at first appears to be the fanciful cupola of some long-collapsed, grand hotel, but if you walk to it, you'll find a pavilion under a spreading curved dome, sort of an offshoot of the Karelian Victorian architectural style of the North Conway railway station. The spring still fills the pool in its center, and the place stands dilapidated and overgrown; near where the road enters the field, you'll find some foundations of a guest house, really a large farmhouse, and a building where the water was bottled.

The *Mt. Washington Observatory Resource Center,* on Route 16 in North Conway, is a good stop if you can't make it to the summit of Mt. Washington. The center has exhibits on the history and work of the observatory, the Summit Road, the Cog Railway, the mountain hotels, and local hiking. Students of the mountains will find the center's collection of rare books, magazines, and pamphlets an invaluable resource. Exhibits are open daily 9:00 A.M. to 5:00 P.M., May 15 to October 15; the library is open Thursdays only. Write them at P.O. Box 2310, North Conway 03860; telephone (603) 356–8345.

In Intervale, back on Route 16, is a scenic overlook with a fine panorama of the mountains and Cathedral Ledge. Opposite is Intervale Crossroad, right beside the post office. Only about 100 yards up this road on your left, you will see a little cabin and a stone with a bronze plaque. Park and cross the railroad to the *Abenaki Encampment and Shop.* Each summer, from 1884 until 1964, members of the Abenaki tribe came from their winter home in Quebec to Cathedral Woods, where they camped and traded with guests of the White Mountain hotels, who visited the encampment to watch the Abenaki weave baskets, which made fine souvenirs. Stephen Laurent, son of the Abenaki chief who started the encampment, still owns the property and the little shop that has been in use there since the late nineteenth century.

The Case of the Missing Tourist Attraction

*I*n the heyday of the grand hotels—from the Civil War to the end of the century—guests arrived by train and stayed for weeks, so it was up to the hotels to amuse them. Each day, they offered excursions, and one of the favorites near Conway was a circuit that stopped first at Echo Lake, then at the gigantic Washington Boulder, and then at White Mountain Mineral Springs in Redstone. The wooden springhouse, as you know, is still there, but not a trace remains of the presumably more durable Washington Boulder. Despite its having been named for the "Father of his Country," it was quarried in 1900, and you can see it now in neat blocks as the foundation to the public library in Conway, at the intersection of Routes 113 and 16.

Abenaki Encampment

Go when you can spend some time to hear the stories of this Abenaki scholar, who is continuing his father's life work of writing a dictionary of the Abenaki language. Along with sweetgrass baskets, beadwork, and Nemadji earth pottery, there are publications on Indian culture for sale. An authentic birchbark wigwam stands nearby under majestic pine trees. The shop, which is listed on the National Register of Historic Places, is open daily from June 15 to October 15, 10:00 A.M. to noon and 3:00 to 5:00 P.M.

Running parallel to often-busy Route 16 through Intervale is Route 16A, which was bypassed by the new road. Now a quiet residential byway, the road was once lined with inns and hotels. A few remain, among them *The Forest Inn,* which has hosted travelers continuously since it opened in 1890. Today its rooms are furnished in lovingly restored antiques; rooms on the top floor have recessed windows set inside the slope of the mansard roof. It's the kind of inn where guests gather in the evening to share experiences with the lively innkeepers. Perhaps the spirit of the place is best described in the attitude of this hospitable couple: "Spending time with our guests is what makes this business fun." Groomed cross-country ski trails begin at the door and downhill skiing is minutes away. Don't plan an early start, however, since breakfast is well worth lingering over. The Forest is part of *"Bike the Whites"* and a similar cross-country ski package with two other inns (see page 155). Write to The Forest at P.O. Box 37, Intervale 03845; telephone (800) 448–3534.

Wildcat Valley

Tucked into a corner, away from the hustle to the south, is the village of Jackson, with its red covered bridge and white church. Artists discovered its scenic beauty in the mid-1800s, and by the turn of the century, Jackson had twenty-four lodging places, including several grand hotels. By the late 1970s, only Eagle Mountain House and a few smaller guest houses were still operating.

But this story has a happier ending than most. Today a number of these have reopened, including the Victorian treasure, Wentworth Hall. Not all of its original thirty-nine buildings could be saved from years of neglect and abandonment, but the three central ones and several other cottages with their curved porches, round towers, wide gables, and quirky architectural detail are once again the showpiece of the village center.

The **Wentworth Resort** is just as nice inside as it is outside, with real feather pillows, giant bathtubs, and an air of grandeur that is comfortable, not intimidating. Rooms in the Arden, Wildwood, and Amster cottages are unique, taking advantage of the architecture of each. In the main building, the Thornycroft suite is our favorite, with its carefully restored antiques, custom-built bed, window seat, and sleigh settee, its marble fireplace, and even a fireplace in the ample Jacuzzi room.

The dining room is just as memorable; the menu is innovative, but not just for the sake of being different. Each season brings new dishes as the chef takes advantage of the freshest ingredients. Smoked duck breast may be served on a bed of grilled red onions, onion soup laced with cider and cheddar, veal topped with morels and brandy, or quail stuffed with wild rice and cashews, as we would expect from a chef with such a careful eye to detail. The public is invited to dine here but should call to make reservations. The hotel is open year-round. Write the Wentworth Resort Hotel, Box M, Jackson 03846; call (603) 383–9700 or (800) 637–0013.

A short walk up the road is **_Jackson Falls,_** a series of cascades with potholes that invite jumping into, if the weather is only halfway nice. The hotel has a pool, of course, but these falls must have been the original inspiration for water slides. There is a circular route of 6 miles (called, for some reason, the Five Mile Drive) that begins at the Wentworth and goes up the Carter Notch Road past the falls. Instead of continuing to the top of the notch (where the road turns into a trail), turn right and cross the river for views across highland meadows to the mountains.

Black Mountain Ski Area is usually forgotten in the razzmatazz of its bigger neighbors, but this end-of-the-road place is a favorite of anyone who has ever skied there. Skiing on Black Mountain has been synonymous with ***Whitney's*** since "Ma" Whitney bought the old Moody Farm in 1936 and welcomed skiers to the first overhead ski lift in the East on Black Mountain, literally out her back door. The lift was made from Sears Roebuck shovel handles. Generations of skiers later, ***Whitney's Inn Jackson*** still welcomes skiers, Black Mountain has grown into a full-service ski area whose lift rates are one of the best ski values in the White Mountains, and "Ma" Whitney has retired to a house on the edge of the slopes above the inn. Comfortable rooms, a hearty breakfast, and special facilities and programs for children make Whitney's popular with families. It's a year-round resort as well, with special summer packages that include a Wednesday night lobster cookout. Whitney's address is Post Office Box W, Route 16B, Jackson 03846; telephone (603) 383–8916 or (800) 677–5737.

Cross-country skiing is an art form in Jackson. This is the home of the ***Jackson Ski Touring Foundation,*** which maintains 150 kilometers of exceptionally well-groomed trails throughout the village and all over the surrounding hillsides. In winter, with no leaves to obscure the view, the neighboring mountains, including the southern slopes of Mount Washington, are visible from every hillside. It's so beautiful on a crisp winter day that it's hard to concentrate on skiing.

Just high enough above the center of Jackson Village to give it a full view of Mt. Washington, *The Inn at Thorn Hill* was designed by Stanford White and built in 1895. Its Victorian legacy is nicely preserved; guest rooms are individually decorated, although the views from nearly every window would be decoration enough. Like Sugar Hill in the western White Mountains, Jackson is a small town that looms large on the culinary map, and the inn's outstanding dining room eclipses even the views. Rarely have we been offered a selection so difficult to choose from—a galette of smoked tomato, pancetta, basil, and parmesan and a smoked trout and grilled pear salad were two of the starter selections we ordered before we even reached the entrees. Four-course dinners are included in the room rate, or served to nonguests at a fixed price of $28. Along with direct access to the network of cross-country trails and proximity to four ski areas, the inn offers tobogganing on the property, even at night. Art and photography workshops with artists from Cape Ann are a long-standing tradition at the inn, which can be reached at Thorn Hill Road, Post Office Box A, Jackson Village 03846; telephone (603) 383–4242 or (800) 289–8990.

Heritage New Hampshire isn't just another theme park—in fact, it's not a theme park at all. It's the life work of a family with a dream. What it lacks in the latest gimmickry, it makes up for in sheer Yankee ingenuity, and you'll have fun figuring out how they do achieve the effects. You leave an English street to board a tossing ship for the New World and land in New Hampshire. The stage thus set, you travel through the history of the state, which is pretty much the history of America. Your kids—and you—will learn about the native peoples, the early use of water power, the King's Pines, the land grants, Portsmouth shipbuilding, the Concord Coach, Daniel Webster (try to figure out how his face moves as he speaks), town meetings, and go for a train ride and leave with a haunting image of the Amoskeag Mills. Heritage New Hampshire is in Glen on Route 16 and is open mid-May to mid-October; (603) 383–9776.

Near the top of Pinkham Notch on Route 16 is a trio of short, rewarding hikes. Look for the parking area for *Glen Ellis Falls* on the west side of the road. This short walk, beginning at the tunnel under the highway, leads to the cliff-lined Ellis River, which plunges over cascades and then through a narrow cleft in the granite, falling 65 feet into a basin before continuing through its boulder-strewn bed.

The Appalachian Mountain Club Visitor Center, just up the road, is the starting point for the ½-mile walk to *Lost Pond.* Cross Route 16 to the east side. The trail crosses a bridge then runs south for ½-mile to the pond. While the falls shows the wild side of nature, this shallow pond shows a gentler, more tranquil wilderness. At the southern end is a beaver dam and a jumble of boulders, dropped here from the slopes above. In dry weather the path continues on to Glen Ellis Falls. You can get your

National Forest permit here, but note that if you park here for Glen Ellis Falls, you don't need a pass. If you park in the area at the falls, you do.

Crystal Cascade is an easy fifteen-minute walk up the trail behind the Visitor Center, following the Cutler River upstream. Although called a cascade, this is really a falls, the water dropping almost vertically 60 feet into a deep chasm and then falling another 20 feet. We have always felt that the best place to view a waterfall is facing its midpoint, a vantage usually reserved for winged creatures. But the unique bend in the river provides an overlook at exactly the right point for viewing this one.

A wide variety of programs and classes are held by the ***Appalachian Mountain Club*** at the Pinkham Notch Visitors Center. These go on year-round and include nature, mountaineering, hiking, botany, photography, fly tying, winter survival, and other subjects. Some are free evening programs, others day or weekend classes that require advance registration and include lodging. For a complete schedule, contact them at P.O. Box 298, Gorham, 03581; (603) 466–2727.

A bit farther up Route 16, at the head of Pinkham Notch, you'll find the entrance to the ***Mt. Washington Auto Road***, opposite the site of the long-gone Glen House, one of the grand hotels. Its carriage houses remain, and in them you can see some of the vehicles that have carried passengers up the scenic road since its building: the first coach, two wagons, a Pierce Arrow, and a wood-paneled Beach Wagon. In the wagon days, they had to replace all the brakes entirely after each trip down the mountain. You can drive along the road in your own car or ride up in one of the fleet of new vans with a guide who'll point out everything from historic sites to the unusual geologic formations beside the road.

Nearby is **Great Glen Trails**, a new facility for cross-country skiing, snowshoeing, and ice skating in the winter and for walking and bicycling in other seasons. They offer guided nature walks, archery, a concert series, barbecues and kite flying. Bike rentals include helmets, and you can even rent a kid's trailer to pull along behind as you jog or bike. In the winter, they rent all kinds of sports equipment, including kick sleds, popular in Finland but rare here; (603) 466–2333.

Mount Washington

At just over a mile high, Mount Washington is the highest mountain in the northeast, but its weather conditions are among the most severe in the world. Arctic equipment is tested at its summit. Only sightly below it stand other mountains named for presidents—thus the name "Presidential Range."

Crawford Notch, a break in the almost solid chain of the White Mountains, lies due south of Mount Washington. Geologically, the notch is a classic glacial scour. During the Ice Age, boulders frozen into the ice caught onto chunks of loose bedrock as the glacier moved down mountain slopes. In valleys, where the action of the glacier became more concentrated, the scouring was at its greatest, carrying off boulders and pieces of broken cliffs which in turn scraped even deeper as they moved, giving a characteristic U-shaped curve to the valley walls.

In the early days of settlement, vast forests of very tall trees covered all but the tops of the mountains, so the settlers couldn't tell where the notches and the passes were. About all they could do was follow the riverbeds, hoping to find the easiest and lowest route.

Usually, these routes were discovered more or less by accident. So it was with Timothy Nash the day he climbed a tree on Cherry Mountain while moose hunting and saw the gap in the line of mountains. He went to Portsmouth to ask the royal governor (the same Benning Wentworth we met earlier) for a piece of land and a road through the notch. The governor told him to bring a horse through the notch, which Timothy and a friend did by lowering it over the cliff on a rope. Nash got his land, and eventually the road was built, opening a much shorter route to the north country.

The trees that filled the notch, like those of the Passaconaway Valley, fell to the lumber market. Entire towns sprang up around the lumber camps, and some of them died with the industry. *Livermore,* a ghost town today, lies along Sawyer River Road, which meets Route 302 just north of the bridge over the Sawyer River about 5 miles north of Bartlett. A mile and a half up Sawyer River Road you'll see a barred gate and some foundations, which are all that is left of Livermore. It was once a thriving community of 200, built in the late 1800s and reached by both road and railroad. Of its homes, stores, boardinghouses, offices, and two saw-mills, you'll find only ruins. Walk to the river and into the woods upstream to find cellar holes and the ruins of a beautifully constructed concrete and brick sawmill. All of these have full-sized trees growing out of them now. It's easier to find the cellar holes in the fall when the leaves are missing. Look for the one with the company safe clearly visible.

Just north of the Sawyer River Road is the **Notchland Inn,** a granite mansion that has been a Crawford Notch landmark since its construction in 1862. The front parlor of this Victorian home was designed by Gustav Stickley; an adjoining country schoolhouse has been transformed into two suites. Guests can join a guided walk to a dramatic gorge and swimming hole located on the property or, in winter, go for a sleigh ride. The Notchland Inn is on Route 302, Harts Location 03812; call (603) 374–6131 or (800) 866–6131.

At the "head" of the notch is a narrow gateway and the **old train station** where the summer guests arrived, bound for the Crawford House Hotel, which once stood guard over the notch. The hotel is gone, but the little Victorian station is an Appalachian Mountain Club (AMC) information center, where you can get trail maps and advice if you plan to do any serious climbing.

The happy news is that with the reopening of the railroad through the notch, trains arrive once more, and if you check the schedule of the Conway Scenic Railroad, you can be there to see one come through the "Gateway to the Notch" and pull up to the station. Better yet, you can be on one (see page 181).

Less than half a mile behind the railway station is a waterfall where the Abolitionist Henry Ward Beecher liked to swim, so it was named **Beecher's Falls,** after him. Follow the Avalon Trail across the tracks and over Crawford Brook. Shortly beyond, a side trail to the left

Author's Note

As a child, tucked into my sleeping bag on summer nights beside the Ammonoosuc River, my sleep was sometimes interrupted by the long, mournful whistle of the train as it passed almost over my head on its way between Fabyan Station and Twin Mountain. But I never rode it farther north than Conway. Later, after the train line was abandoned—forever, everyone thought—we walked the tracks, but only as far as the trestle, where the land dropped straight down into the notch. The track was deteriorating, and it was too late to ride the train through the notch as I had dreamed of doing on those long ago nights.

Last summer I rode that train I thought was gone forever, through the notch and past the scenes of childhood summers— past Notchland with its strange stone house where there used to be a thank-you-marm in the road, over trails I'd climbed to waterfalls, and over the trestle where I still didn't dare to look down. When the train came through the rocks at the Gateway to the Notch, I half expected to see Crawford House, a phoenix arisen from its ashes like the railroad. Even if it had been there, I wouldn't have been able to see it through the tears. You CAN go home again.

—*Barbara Radcliffe Rogers*

climbs a very short way to the falls. The brook channels through a narrow chute and drops about 25 feet into a pool below. Follow the brook upstream to a second falls, and then to a third.

The best view of Crawford Notch is down into it from *Mount Willard,* an easy climb (more accurately, an uphill walk) along an old bridle path to the summit. From there you can see the great scoop of the notch

Stables at Bretton Arms

below you, as well as the shimmering cascades that fall off the mountains through rocky ravines. Watch overhead for peregrine falcons, which have nesting sites near the summit of Mount Willard.

Past Saco Lake, which is the source of the Saco River, is Mount Clinton Road, which leads to *Jefferson Notch.* Possibly the least known of the White Mountain notches, its 3,009-foot elevation is the highest point in the state reached by a public road. Gravel all the way, the road passes through deep woods along Monroe Brook, which cascades over rocks between moss-covered banks. At the top, the forest is still too tall to allow any panoramic views, but drive into the parking lot for a good, close view of Mount Washington's summit, 3,000 feet above you. The road descends into the town of Jefferson; the entire trip is 9 miles.

While the Cog Railway to the summit of Mount Washington is one of the state's best known attractions, the new *Cog Railway Museum* at the base station enjoys less celebrity. Located opposite the ticket window on the ground floor, its displays include cutaway versions of an early coach and boiler, showing how these were originally built and how they worked. There are also exhibits on the mountain's unusual weather, the history of the railway, and other related subjects. There is an admission charge, except for those who hold tickets for the train. The museum is open daily May through October. Telephone (603) 846–5404 or (800) 922–8825, ext. 5.

While the *Mount Washington Hotel* is a White Mountain landmark, few know the *Bretton Arms,* a former chauffeur's quarters that served as home to the Secretariat during the Bretton Woods Monetary Conference in 1944. Now an inn and a National Historic Landmark, the Bretton Arms offers newly renovated guest rooms and a more intimate atmosphere than the grand hotel up the hill. Be sure to see the magnificent Victorian stable building just past the inn, where horses, sleighs, and carriages are still housed. The Bretton Arms is located next to the cross-country ski center at Bretton Woods 03575; telephone (603) 278–1000 or (800) 258–0330.

The dining room at the Bretton Arms is small and intimate. The menu, too, is different, making the most of opportunities the grand hotel's large dining room doesn't have. Try as we might to sample different starters, we can't resist the smoked duck with cheddar walnut ravioli. If wild boar in mountain berry plum sauce is on the menu, don't miss it.

The **Mount Washington Hotel** exudes the opulence of its era, as it should, and it's been restored by owners who really care about the details. (They studied old photos and sent to England for replicas of the original Axminster lobby carpets.) It also exudes history. Nearly every nook and cranny has its story, many of which involve The Princess. The hotel's first owner died only a few years after its opening, and his widow remarried a European prince. They continued to return to the hotel for summers, living in Paris in the winter, and she had her magnificent bed crated and shipped with her twice each year. The Princess's bed, now retrofitted to queen (Why does this strike us funny?), is in an Executive room at the hotel, with a Jacuzzi the Princess would have had crated up and shipped to France each winter, too, had it been here then. Speaking of Jacuzzis, room 114 has one in its bay window nook overlooking the mountains. The Mount Washington Hotel is in Bretton Woods 03589; (603) 278–1000 or (800) 258–0330.

While you can argue that the hotel is not off the beaten path, the three free tours they give certainly are. You don't have to be a hotel guest to join; just ask at the activities desk. Each of the staff members who leads them has different stories to tell—perhaps of The Princess sitting behind a curtain in a little balcony watching the ladies descend to the dining room each evening before choosing which gown to wear to dinner—but you'll certainly see the Tiffany windows and the table where the Bretton Woods Monetary

Agreement was signed, and find out why the dining room is round.

The other tours take you to the print shop, where the menus are still hand set in type each day and printed on a press the Smithsonian wants, and to the Stickney Chapel, where one of the windows is signed by Louis Comfort Tiffany and the others are made by his students. If you can, go on a sunny afternoon when the sun is backlighting the chapel's front window.

The Kind of Ghost You Like to Have Around

I was staying at the Mount Washington Hotel with our daughter, who was at the time about eight years old; it was a warm evening, and we left our big windows open to sleep in the fresh mountain air. In the morning the windows were firmly closed. Odd, I thought, but I said nothing. The next night, the same thing happened, and in the morning I mentioned it to Julie, who not only sleeps like a granite boulder but was too short to have reached the windows. She suggested that the window might simply have slipped down, but when I checked, the balance and suspension were perfect, and the windows stayed exactly where I put them. "Must be the ghost of the Princess," Julie laughed.

When the housekeeping staff came to do up the room, I mentioned the windows. Without so much as a twinkle in her eye, the woman said quite matter-of-factly, "She was probably afraid the little girl would get up in the night and fall through the screen, so she shut them." After that, we left the windows down and saved the Princess that stop on her nightly rounds of her hotel.

—Barbara Radcliffe Rogers

For another view of the Mount Washington Hotel and of the mountain and valley, have dinner at the top of Bretton Woods Ski Area's quad chairlift. You can ride up to dinner at **Top o' Quad Restaurant** (and get a free ticket for a daytime trip) or take the restaurant's van to the top. The menu offers a good variety, but it has to compete with the view. If you're lucky, you'll be there shortly after an evening thunder shower, as we were recently, in time to see a giant rainbow drop into the valley, straight into the Mount Washington Hotel. Did we have a camera with us? Of course not. Dinner is served Wednesday through Saturday, from the end of June through Columbus Day weekend; call (603) 278–5000 or (800) 232–2972.

The ski area, by the way, is a favorite with families for its kid-friendly programs.

Instead of leaving the area via Jefferson Notch, you can continue along Route 302 to the Zeeland Campground, where there is a nice picnic area along the Ammonoosuc River. If you continue up the Zeeland Road, about 3½ miles to its end, you can take the Zeeland Trail to **Zeeland Falls,** a 2½-mile, easy hike. Getting to the top of the falls is the only climbing involved—there is only about a 350-foot difference in altitude from the parking lot to the top of the falls. The falls is really a cascade, and at its top, from the AMC hut, is a view of New Hampshire's hidden notch. Only hikers can see the dramatic shape of Zeeland Notch, for no road penetrates it at any point. Take a lunch to eat by the falls as you enjoy the view. Along the trail you will follow the bed of a nineteenth-century logging railroad and pass through hardwood forests. It's hard to picture this entire valley laid waste by uncontrolled lumbering and the resulting fire and erosion damage, so great was the ability of the forest to rejuvenate itself here.

About halfway up the Zealand Road is the **Sugarloaf Campground,** one of the loveliest and most secluded in the mountains. Roomy sites are carved out of young forest, some with direct paths to the rocky Zealand River below. Resident hosts, a lively couple who have camped here for more than thirty years, occupy a central campsite all summer and can tell you where the best fishing and blueberrying are. For information, write to the District Ranger, White Mountain National Forest, Bethlehem 03574.

The **Twin Mountain Fish and Wildlife Center**, on Route 3 north of Twin Mountain, has a museum featuring local wildlife and an excellent exhibit on "Water on the Move." It shows water in all its habitats, in a flowing stream, a riffle area, cold water pool, beaver pond, and wetland, each with its fish life. Although we think it was intended for kids, we found it fascinating, and we learned a lot about our finny neighbors. You can also tour the hatchery and hike a nature trail. It's free and open daily, 9:00 A.M. to 4:30 P.M.; call (603) 846–5108.

PLACES TO STAY
IN THE EASTERN WHITE MOUNTAINS
(ALL AREA CODES 603)

WATERVILLE VALLEY
The Valley Inn, Waterville Valley 03215; 236–8336 or (800) GO–VALLEY. A full-service hotel with the warmth of an inn, moderate prices, and some real bargain specials. The restaurant offers an innovative menu in an attractive candlelit setting. We hardly ever order steak, but their Steak Horatio, with crab, asparagus, and bearnaise lures us every time.

Black Bear Lodge, 03215; 236–8383 or (800) GO–VALLEY. Two-room suites with kitchenettes. Ideal for families, with pool in building and moderate rates.

CAMPTON
Mountain-Fare Inn, Mad River Road, Campton 03223; 726–4283. An 1840s village house with antiques and flower gardens; moderately priced.

NORTH CONWAY
The Farm by the River, 2555 West Side Road, 03860; 356–2694 or (888) 414–8353. An original land-grant farm, still in the same family since King George III. Horses, cross-country skiing, and fishing on the property.

Green Granite Resort, Route 16, 356–6901 or (800) 468–3666. Family owned, and one of the most attractive, hospitable lodgings in town, with indoor heated and outdoor pools, an exercise room, and sauna. Doubles $99–$120, including breakfast.

LINCOLN
Mountain Club at Loon, Loon Mountain Resort, 03251; 745–3441 or (800) 229–STAY. A modern hotel that keeps the atmosphere of a ski lodge; indoor parking, balconies, pools. Rates $80–$190.

GORHAM
Appalachian Mountain Club, Route 16, 03581; 466–2727. The Pinkham Notch Visitors Center offers rustic lodging and three meals a day at reasonable prices.

GLEN
The Bernerhof, Route 302, 03838; 383–4414 or (800) 548–8007. Small hotel and European dining room, with a "Taste of the Mountains Cooking School" weekends. Entrees are $15–$21.

JACKSON

Christmas Farm Inn, Route 16B, 03846; 383–4313 or (800) HI–ELVES. Fine country inn; rates include breakfast and dinner.

PLACES TO EAT
IN THE EASTERN WHITE MOUNTAINS
(ALL AREA CODES 603)

THORNTON

Bridge House Inn, Route 49, 726–9853. Dinner Wednesday–Sunday and brunch on weekends.

WATERVILLE VALLEY

Chile Peppers, Town Square, 236–4646. Mexican dishes, well prepared, at moderate prices.

LINCOLN

Cafe Lafayette Dinner Train, Hobo Railroad Station, 745–3500 or (800) 699–3501. A restored, 1952 Pullman Dome Car travels at a stately speed along the Pemigewasset Valley while passengers enjoy dinner and a changing panorama. It runs Wednesday through Sunday evenings between Memorial Day and Columbus Day, with a few runs late in the fall and again before Christmas.

NORTH WOODSTOCK

Woodstock Station, 80 Main Street, 745–3951. Busy for three meals a day during the summer, look for off-season dining bargains. Live entertainment nightly and an adjacent brewpub. Entrees are $8.00–$14.00

NORTH CONWAY

The Ledges, White Mountain Hotel, West Side Road, 356–7100. Serves three meals daily from a varied menu, with an excellent wine list. Entrees $10–$16.

The Western White Mountains

The summer social season on this side of the White Mountains involved not only guests at the grand hotels—Profile House, Forest Hills, Sunset Hill, and the resorts of Bethlehem—but an increasing number of wealthy people who built their own summer estates, especially in Sugar Hill and Bethlehem. When the era of hotel summers ended, these families continued to return. Some retired here, giving the area a permanent cultural tradition that shows today in regular art and music events.

This land is beautiful and the mountains a little less craggy than the Presidential Range to the east. Towns here have less of a seasonal air about them, being year-round communities with their own economic base. Downtown stores cater more to local needs than to tour-bus shopping expeditions. Hospitality is warm, and visitors return to the same inn year after year.

Country stores, covered bridges, farms, and mountain streams punctuate the miles of forests bordering the winding country roads. Only the stone walls that wind through the woodlands remind us that much of this land was once cleared for farming. This is a place for relaxing, exploring, and savoring.

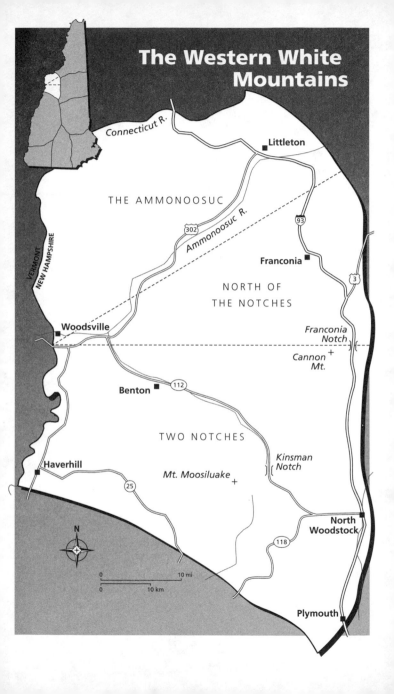

The Western White Mountains

Connecticut R.

Littleton

THE AMMONOOSUC

302

Ammonoosuc R.

93

Franconia

3

NORTH OF
THE NOTCHES

VERMONT

NEW HAMPSHIRE

Woodsville

Franconia
Notch

Cannon
Mt.

112

Benton

TWO NOTCHES

Kinsman
Notch

Haverhill

25

Mt. Moosiluake

North
Woodstock

118

N

0   10 mi
0   10 km

Plymouth

THE WESTERN WHITE MOUNTAINS' TOP PICKS

Kinsman Notch

Agaziz Basin

Lost River

Old Man of the Mountain

Cascade Brook and Kinsman Falls

New England Ski Museum

The Rim Trail

Sugar Hill Historical Museum

Hilltop Inn

North Country Chamber Players

Sunset Hill House

Franconia iron furnace

Robert Frost Place

The Rocks

Bretzfelder Memorial Park

Adair and Tim-Bir Alley Restaurant

Maplewood

Newt Washburn

Wallace Horse Cemetery

Littleton Historical Museum

Kilburn Crags

Bath Village Bridge

Upper Village

Two Notches

The White Mountain National Forest's westernmost segment begins just south of Sugar Hill and Franconia. Route 116 continues past the Frost Place to the town of Easton, high in the hills and completely surrounded by the national forest. South of Easton on Route 112 is a wild and beautiful notch almost completely overshadowed by the fame of neighboring Franconia Notch.

The road through **Kinsman Notch** winds and curves and climbs until it reaches tiny Beaver Lake, a high mountain tarn, rockbound and icy cold. In its center rises a rocky, pine-clad island. The landscape here is wild and almost desolate under the slope of Mount Blue—but nowhere near as forbidding as it must have looked to Asa Kinsman and his wife. With their household goods on a two-wheeled cart pulled by oxen, they discovered that they had taken the wrong track to their new home in Landaff. Instead of turning back to go around the mountains that lay in their way, they hacked a path through the notch. If you take a turn you didn't plan on or miss the road you wanted, just remember the Kinsmans and take heart.

At its top the notch opens out, giving excellent views down the valley to the east. The narrowness and curves of the road at the top give a real sense of this being a pass, more so than some of the better-known notches. (You may notice that the state highway map has the Kinsman Notch label a little to the east of its actual location 6 miles from North Woodstock.)

For some reason we can't understand, **Agaziz Basin** is never listed among the natural attractions of the White

Authors' Favorite Attractions/Events in the Western White Mountains

The Old Man of the Mountain and The Flume, Franconia Notch

The Aerial Tramway, Franconia (603) 823–5563

Lost River Gorge, North Woodstock (603) 745–8031

Clark's Trading Post, North Woodstock (603) 745–8913

Ski Areas: *Waterville, Loon Mountain, Cannon Mountain*

Frostbite Follies, mid-February, Franconia (603) 823–5661, (800) 237–9007

Lilac Time Festival, late May, Lisbon (603) 838–6336

Fields of Lupine Festival, mid-late June, Sugar Hill and Franconia (603) 823–5661, (800) 237–9007

July Fourth Festival, Littleton (603) 444–6561

Music in the White Mountains Summer Festival, July-August, Lincoln and Sugar Hill (603) 869–3154

Quilt Festival, mid-October, Sugar Hill and Franconia (603) 823–5661, (800) 237–9007

Mountains, whereas less interesting gorges and waterfalls are. It's also easier than most to get to, right beside Route 112, just west of North Woodstock. In the summer, there's a sign; off-season, look for *Gavoni's Restaurant* (a good choice for traditional Italian dishes). They share a parking lot. One of the safer of New England's gorges to visit, there's a bridge over the falls.

Lost River really isn't lost, it just plays hide and seek for a while among glacially jumbled boulders, falling into huge rock chambers and through caves. Boardwalks and stairs make the trip easier, and you can simply walk through, or you can wriggle through the "lemon squeezer" or other tight passages that the claustrophobic should probably avoid. It's a beautiful area, and at the top is a garden with examples of woodland wildflowers, some of them quite rare. You can see the garden without paying the $7.00 admission to go through Lost River. Open mid-May to late October 9:00 A.M. to 5:00 P.M., until 6:00 P.M. in July and August. It's on Route 112 in Kinsman Notch; (603) 745–8031.

Franconia Notch is one of the most frequently visited spots in New Hampshire, and it is the home of the state's symbol, the *Old Man of the Mountain.* It was to protect the fragile ledges of this famous stone profile from the dangers of blasting that Interstate 93 was stopped just below the notch and resumed just above it. It took a U.S. congressman with the courage to dig in his heels and take on the whole of Washington, but the integrity of the notch was saved, and its hidden treasures remain in seclusion despite the number of visitors at its famous attractions. A bicycle path runs the length of the notch, crossing the highway through specially built underpasses.

The new *Old Man of the Mountain Museum* is at the head of Franconia Notch, where the paths to Echo Lake begin. In it are interpretive materials on the profile and its history, including a collection of souvenirs that have borne its likeness over the years.

A trail from the glacial formation known as the Basin leads to *Cascade Brook and Kinsman Falls.* Although these cascades are not ten minutes' level walk from the Basin, they are never crowded and provide a fine place to picnic or just explore. The ledges over which the brook slides and drops have been worn into graceful curves, potholes, tiny flumes, and gorges by the brook. In places the water spreads over the granite in a smooth sheet; elsewhere it falls in ribbons from pool to pool. You can climb through the woods along the trail or up the sloping face of the ledges. When water is high or the weather rainy, it's better to stay on the trail and avoid the slippery rocks.

At the head of the notch, by the base of the Aerial Tramway, is the *New England Ski Museum.* Permanent and changing exhibits tell the story of this sport with historical equipment, photographs, art, and even changing fashions in skiwear. Open daily December 26 to March 31, 11:00 A.M. to 4:00 P.M., and Memorial Day weekend to October 15, noon to 5:00 P.M.; the admission is free. Write The New England Ski Museum, P.O. Box 267, Franconia 03580; call (603) 823–7177.

Authors' Note

*T*he Old Man of the Mountain (no "s" at the end, please) shouldn't be there. The top two of the five granite ledges that form the great stone face are cantilevered out well beyond the carrying capacity of the distance for which they penetrate the mountainside. "There's nothing holding them up; they should have fallen into the notch centuries ago," says the man who knows these famous ledges better than anyone else. Niels Nielsen climbed down over the old man's face, suspended on ropes, every year from 1960 to the 1980s, when his son David took over the job, to measure slippage and seal any cracks that might allow water to freeze inside and split the ledge. Equipment for this annual face lift is brought up by helicopter; the Nielsens are volunteers, and the first time David went down the face, he was 11 years old.

The Rim Trail can be reached from the top of the Aerial Tramway (look for one of its original 1930s cars at the Ski Museum) or via the Kinsman Ridge trail from the head of Franconia Notch. It offers hikers panoramic views into the notch and across the Franconia and Presidential ranges along the exposed rim and from the observation tower at the end. Notice the scar on the steep facing slope of Mount Lafayette, caused by a 1959 landslide that covered the road through the notch with 27 feet of debris. Even today, the physical forces of weathering and erosion continue the work of the glaciers in changing the landscape of the notches. Be sure to watch for peregrine falcons that nest on Eagle Cliff, below, where golden eagles once laid their eggs.

North of the Notches

Over the hills, on Route 117, lies Sugar Hill, stretched along the top of a ridge overlooking some of the White Mountains' most beautiful scenery. It's the kind of genteel town where people wave to you from their front porches as you go for an evening walk. *Harman's Store* should be your first stop, for fine aged cheddar that bears no resemblance to the grocery store stuff. Harman's sends cheese and first-run New Hampshire maple syrup to people all over the country who don't really believe that there is a town named Sugar Hill. The secret of their cheese is that they buy fine cheddar and then age it themselves. You'll find New Hampshire jams and jellies, soldier beans, common crackers, and whole-wheat pancake flour here, too, and all grades of the New Hampshire maple syrup that gave

Sugar Hill its name. They also sell Vermont syrup for those people who won't believe that maple trees grow all over New England, New York, and Quebec (but the proprietors snicker a little behind their counter when they do). Open year-round daily, May to October, closed Sundays November to April. Call Harman's Cheese and Country Store at (603) 823–8000.

Across the street is the *Historical Museum.* Housed in three buildings, the exhibits show, through an exceptional collection of old photographs, artifacts, carriages, and furnishings, the daily life of early settlers and Sugar Hill's heyday as a summer resort. Here are the kitchen from a stagecoach tavern with its original furnishings, a blacksmith shop, the ornate wagon of a local hotel, and a genealogical library. Admission is only $2.00 ($1.00 for seniors and children ages twelve or older). Open from July 1 through late October, Thursday, Saturday, and Sunday, 1:00 to 4:00 P.M. (603–823–8142).

Within walking distance of both of these is *Hilltop Inn.* This is one of those places that friends hesitate to tell you about because they are afraid it will become so popular that there won't be room for them. The 1895 Victorian home is decorated with period furniture but offers every modern comfort. Big beds, plenty of pillows for late-night readers, flannel sheets, and antique linens are just a few of the luxuries. But the real charm of the Hilltop Inn is its owners, Meri and Mike Hern. Their offbeat sense of humor and irrepressible enthusiasm make old friends out of strangers from the first rumble of Mike's contagious chuckle.

In the back of the property is a cottage almost dwarfed by its gardens—roses along the fence, primroses and achillea. It has a full modern kitchen, but guests have breakfast in the main house. (No one in his right mind would miss one of Meri's breakfasts.) It's nice for families or for a bit more room and privacy on a longer stay. Write Hilltop Inn, Main Street, Sugar Hill 03585; call (603) 823–5695.

Since its heyday as a summer resort, Sugar Hill has had a flourishing arts community and hosts the **North Country Chamber Players** annual summer festival in the Meeting House on Friday evenings in July and August. Members of this organization hold first-chair positions in major orchestras. For a complete schedule of concerts write Box 99, Franconia 03580 or call (603) 869–3154.

The Road Not Taken

*W*hile exploring the Franconia area, we were staying with our friend Joanie at her Sugar Hill home, the last house on the paved part of her road, which continues on for a distance along the wooded hillside before joining up with another. Her home is lovely, her lawns mowed and her flower gardens impeccable; this is not a falling-down farmhouse, and Joanie is a well-dressed, cosmopolitan lady, even in her garden clothes. Which is how the driver of a car with New Jersey plates found her when he whipped into her yard and asked in an annoyed voice, without even the polite niceties of a "Good Morning," "Where's this road GO, anyway?" Joanie gazed up the road with a slightly puzzled look, as though it hadn't been there last time she looked, smiled very sweetly and said, "I haven't any idea; I've never taken it."

214

Hilltop Inn

The **Sunset Hill House** was one of the grandest of the White Mountain resort hotels, on the crest of a hill with mountain views in all directions. A boardwalk connected it to the village so that ladies could stroll up to watch the sunset without soiling the hems of their gowns. The main building is gone now, but a second one dating from 1882 has just been restored to an opulence that made the original hotel famous. Guest rooms are beautiful and comfortable, with a view from every window. The dining room overlooks the Presidential Range, which on clear evenings is bathed in a rosy reflection of the sunset known as alpen-glow. Dinner guests may have trouble giving the menu the attention it deserves until after dusk claims the mountains, but the flavors of dishes such as chicken and spinach roulade, grilled shrimp with black bean cake, or wild mushroom ravioli with port sauce can

215

compete with any view on equal terms. There is no off-season here, with sleigh rides, cross-country trails, golf, hiking, and maple sugaring available from the front door and ski slopes minutes away. Write Sunset Hill House, Sunset Hill Road, Sugar Hill 03585; telephone (603) 823–5522 or (800) SUNHILL.

In the valley of the Gale River, east of Sugar Hill, Franconia was once the center of an iron industry that thrived from 1811 until the 1850s. The ore came from mines close to Sunset Hill House; the vein was the richest then known. The giant stone *iron furnace* where ore was smelted still stands by the river, near the LaFayette Regional School. An interpretive center and outdoor panels explain the process that turned ore into wrought-iron bars. Inside the building, which is open irregular hours, is a scale model of the furnace, cut away to show its interior. This is the only iron furnace remaining in the state.

South of the village, off Route 116, the *Robert Frost Place* is a small weathered farmhouse, its mailbox marked R. FROST. Along with Robert Frost memorabilia and autographed first editions, there are a slide show, a nature trail marked with lines of his poetry, and a rare collection of the poet's less-known work: Christmas card verses. Open daily 1:00–3:00 P.M., April–October. The Frost Place is in Franconia; call (603) 823–5510.

The Inn at Forest Hills is a beautifully restored "cottage" that was once part of the grand Forest Hills Hotel; it is now a moderately priced B&B. Breakfast is an event. It's at P.O. Box 783, Franconia 03580, or call (603) 823–9550 or (800) 280–9550; fax (603) 823–8701.

The Day the World Didn't End

*T*he Millerites were followers of William Miller, a clergyman of the early 1800s who prophesied the end of the world on October 22, 1844. Sugar Hill had a particularly active group of Millerites, many of whom were so convinced by his preaching that they raised no crops that year, secure in the knowledge that there would be no winter to provide for. Others sold or gave away their livestock as the day approached and devoted themselves to prayer and fasting.

On the ordained day, they gathered at the cemetery on the little rise at the west side of town, which you can see above you as you head toward Lisbon on Route 117. They wore long, flowing white robes, the proper dress for ascending to their eternal reward. The end of the story is probably no surprise to you: The world didn't end on October 22. But locals had a lot of fun over them, especially with one gentleman who was giving his unsaved neighbors a last-minute exhortation that morning and fell asleep afterwards next to a small pile of hay. The objects of his sermon lit the hay on fire and when the man awoke to the smell of smoke and crackling of fire, he was certain the end had come and he'd gone to Hell.

The Ammonoosuc

*B*ethlehem, now a quiet town stretched out along a ridge, was once a major resort capital of the White Mountains. Along its main street stood thirty of the biggest and the grandest hotels, a summer-long procession of splendor and gaiety. They are gone now, but the elegant cottages that surrounded them are still there—some serving today as bed and breakfasts—and so is the pure pollen-free mountain air that attracted the first visitors.

217

Its quiet streets and airy location make Bethlehem a good base for exploring the national forest, where the ban on commercial activity leaves no lodging for those who don't enjoy camping.

There are, it is said, more architectural styles in Bethlehem than in any other New England town. It's easy to believe. But the most unusual must be *The Bells,* a pagoda-shaped three-story cottage on Strawberry Hill Street. For a self-guided tour that reveals some of Bethlehem's lively architectural and social heritage, get a copy of the booklet "An Illustrated Tour of Bethlehem," sold locally for $2.00.

Next to the neoclassical Methodist Church on Main Street is the outlet store for *Nanook Children's Wear.* You've seen these clothes in boutiques and fashionable catalogs, but you've probably never seen them at these prices. Look for the boxes, where you can pull out eyelet party dresses or whatever they have too many of that week. This is a good place to stock up for Christmas. Nanook Children's Wear is on Main Street in Bethlehem (603–869–5761).

The Rocks, west of Bethlehem on Route 302, a late nineteenth-century farm estate, is now in the care of the Society for the Protection of New Hampshire Forests. The double-stone walls, the buttresses, and the lower story of the Victorian barn were built of stones cleared from the rolling pastures and meadows that surround the house and barns. A free leaflet describes the sights along a 2-mile self-guided trail past a highly original sawmill-pigpen and a bee house, and through forest and wetlands.

Another self-guided trail, through the Christmas tree plantations, describes the growing of trees and some of the estate's history, as it leads to a scenic overview.

Seasonal activities are planned on weekends year-round, with a Halloween festival, hay-wagon tours of the Christmas tree plantation (along with cut-your-own sales), a winter forest festival with logging demonstrations, snowshoe tours, maple sugaring, and a wildflower festival. Nature trails and gardens are free and always open; there are fees for special programs, and registration is necessary for some. Write Society for the Protection of New Hampshire Forests, The Rocks, RFD #1, Bethlehem 03574; call (603) 444–6228.

Off Prospect Street and also managed by the same society is the **Bretzfelder Memorial Park,** seventy-seven acres of forest, pond, mountain brook, and picnic area connected by walking and cross-country trails. A leaflet tells about the various trees and signs along the trails explain the natural history and ecology. The story of Mr. Bretzfelder and his favorite tree (the tree is still alive even after major surgery) is told on a sign by the entrance. On Wednesday evenings in July and August at 8:00 P.M., the Evening Rambles explore some aspect of the park—its nocturnal animals, wildflowers, or other subject. No admission is charged; call (603) 444–6228 for dates and a description of the programs.

Just east of the entrance to The Rocks on Route 302, Brook Road leads to Blaney Road, on which stands **Gepetto's Barn,** the workshop of Win Brebner. There he creates toys, furniture, puzzles, castles, chests of blocks, and other useful things of wood. The prices are even more surprising—a good-sized toy box filled with blocks is $50. Doll furniture runs about $3.00. There's no telling what you'll find here; you just have to go and look around. Gepetto's Barn, Blaney Road, Bethlehem 03574, is open Memorial Day weekend to Columbus Day weekend, from morning until dusk. Call (603) 444–2187.

Adair, built in 1927 by Washington D.C. lawyer Frank Hogan, illustrates the popularity of Bethlehem as a summer resort into this century. Family occupied until 1991, this gracious home, set on grounds landscaped by Frederick Law Olmsted, has hosted presidents, Supreme Court justices, and other celebrities. Its new owners have made Adair into an exceptional inn, with elegance, comfort, and noticeable warmth. Original artwork decorates the eight tasteful guest rooms. Spacious parlors and the gardens and lawns of the estate create an atmosphere designed for relaxation. A stay here is well worth the higher-than-average rates. A full breakfast includes several house specialties.

Adair has lured Tim and Biruta Carr, owners of *Tim-Bir Alley* restaurant, to move into the inn's two elegant dining rooms. Formerly in Littleton, Tim-Bir Alley provides an exceptional dining experience. The menu changes daily, featuring at least three entrees, and might start with grilled eggplant and warm goat cheese on roasted red pepper coulis, followed by an entrée of duck breast with fig-almond chutney on pear purée or salmon with fresh basil and garlic-infused olive oil. Local residents would like to keep this restaurant their own secret. Adair and Tim-Bir Alley are off Route 302, just west of The Rocks estate, on Old Littleton Road,

Bethlehem 03574; telephone (603) 444–2600 (fax 444–4823).

Maplewood was not just the largest and grandest of the local hotels; it was a village of its own with Victorian railroad station, farms to provide food for its dining rooms, a sugar bush that yielded one hundred gallons of syrup each spring, a golf course, and a casino with a ballroom, movie theater, and bowling alley. The hotel is gone, but the village of Maplewood is still on the map. The restored casino with its stone tower still guards the golf course and four wonderful old "cottages"—great hulking things with porches and gabled windows—are situated in a row just east of the casino.

Beyond them is a little shrine by the side of the road with a lovely story to tell. From the beginning of the century until 1949, underprivileged boys from a Boston industrial school were brought up in the summers to work as caddies at Maplewood. In 1958, a number of the former caddies, many of them prominent and successful, built the shrine. To this day these men gather at Maplewood for reunions.

Not far from Bethlehem, on its way to Whitefield, Route 142 drops down a long steep hill. At the very bottom, just as the road curves to the left, is the tiny brown workshop of a man who has been honored by the President and whose work is on permanent display at The Smithsonian Institution. *Newt Washburn* is a fourth-generation Abenaki basketmaker, one of fewer than half a dozen who have continued in this art. He designs and makes his own tools, the knives and splitters with which he turns an ash log into a finely woven basket. On a full-sized basket each splint is the thickness of a growth ring separated from the log, but for smaller ones Newt splits each one in half to keep its thickness in proportion to its width. Newt will show you the whole process, from log to basket, and his scrapbook too. Museum-quality Abenaki baskets run from $55 to $100, a real bargain for an original by a craftsman of his reputation. Newt Washburn's workshop is in Bethlehem Hollow (603–869–5894).

Arriving in Littleton on Route 302, *Bishop's Homemade Ice Cream Shoppe* is in a white house on the right. If you can think of any excuse to stop and try this ice cream, do it. You can sit at picnic tables on the lawn or inside the upbeat green-and-white ice cream parlor while you enjoy the old favorite flavors, a wide variety of homemade yogurt flavors, or one of their unique recipes. For calorie watchers or those with cholesterol problems, there are sorbets rich with the taste of real fruit. The Bishop's Bash is filled with chunks of brownie, walnuts, and chocolate chips, and their brandy Alexander ice cream "is as close to the real thing that we serve at our New Year's Eve party as we can get without a liquor license," the owner explains. Open daily from mid-April until mid-October at 78 Cottage Street in Littleton; call (603) 444–6039.

Opposite Bishop's, Mt. Eustice Road travels under Interstate 93, just beyond which a short lane leads to the *Wallace Horse Cemetery.* Inside a small corral are three graves and a family stone; on the fence a placard explains the touching story of the team of matched bay Morgans, buried here with all their regalia, that were the only "children" of the Wallaces from 1889 until the death of the horses in 1919. As touching as the story recounted here are the pennies that visitors have placed on the stones.

Throughout northern New Hampshire you will see photographs of the White Mountains "the way we were" during the Golden Age. Most of these were reproduced from stereoscopic view cards which, when seen through the double lenses of a special viewer, jumped into a three-dimensional landscape or scene. They were the forerunner of the Viewmaster and were a prime source of home entertainment. The major manufacturer of these cards was the Kilburn Brothers Stereoscopic View factory in Littleton.

In the bottom level of the Queen Anne–style Town Building (you can't miss its round, white, four-story tower) is the *Historical Museum.* It contains, along with other local artifacts, an exhibition on the Kilburn stereoscopic views. The museum's new Ammonoosuc Room displays local arts and collections, as well as a scale model of the Mount Willard Section House, a Victorian home that once perched beside the tracks in Crawford Notch. The museum is open Wednesdays from 1:30 to 4:30 P.M.; at other times call (603) 444–6586 for information.

Fossils are not common in New Hampshire, and one of the few places where they are found is atop a rock formation overlooking Littleton. The *Kilburn Crags* are the result of great masses of layered, fossil-bearing rock being heaved into an almost vertical position. The fossils aren't just lying about; it takes some effort to find them, but serious geology buffs may find brachiopods and ferns here. To reach the crags, continue on Route 118 past the Dells (a pleasant picnic area). Half a mile after it separates from Route 135 in a left turn, look for a sign on the left side of the road with a small pull-out for parking. There is no trail, but you can walk along the edge of the field to an old woods road. Follow it to the top, just over half a mile of steady but not difficult climbing. If fossils don't interest you, the view down over Littleton is worth the climb. Watch for moose, which are plentiful here.

Avoid the interstate here by taking Route 18 to the Connecticut River, which forms both the Vermont border and a huge lake behind **Moore Station Dam.** One of the major power-generating dams in the northeast, it has a visitors' center with displays explaining the dam, as well as a picnic area and boat launch on the reservoir. Write the New England Power Company, North Monroe 03771 or call (603) 638–2327.

Route 135 plays hide-and-seek with the Connecticut River through valley farmland to Woodsville. You can either return to the Littleton area on Route 302 or take Route 112 from Bath to Franconia and Kinsman notches.

In Bath be sure to stop at **The Brick Store,** which has been open in the center of town since 1804. Without being "ye olde general store" about it, this emporium manages to retain the feel and much of the merchandise of an old country store while remaining a useful shopping place for local residents. Top shelves are lined with old tins, a thread cabinet, and other vintage store memorabilia, and the home-made fudge is displayed in a glass case. There's a wheel of cheddar on the counter and four shelves of buffalo-plaid wool shirts, a hot item here in the winter. Notice the slanted counter fronts which make room for hoop skirts. If you stop here for a sandwich (if you don't find one you like in the fridge they'll make one up for you), enjoy it sitting on the front porch with a view of Main Street and the old Mobil sign with the red Pegasus.

Behind the store is the **Bath Village Bridge,** a covered bridge so long that motorists are asked to turn on their headlights when entering it. Built in 1832 at a cost of $3,500, it still has its original arches. Be sure to notice its construction (all covered bridges are not built in the same way), a fine example of a Burr arch structure. At 400 feet, it is the longest in New Hampshire and one of the oldest still in use in America.

Bath has two other covered bridges, one of which is just off Route 112 in the village of Swiftwater. Farther along Route 112 and the Wild Ammonoosuc (don't let this confuse you—there are three different Ammonoosuc rivers in the area), where the road parallels the river for a stretch, there is a spot where hopeful prospectors have had moderate luck panning for gold. You may see their vehicles parked along the road. Route 112 leads to Kinsman Notch.

Northeast of Bath on Route 302 is **Upper Village,** a cluster of eight homes remarkable enough to make almost anyone ease up on the gas pedal. The most imposing are three grand brick mansions built in the early 1800s. Also set in the carefully manicured grounds, which cover both sides of the road, are other homes and huge, yellow clapboard barns with steep-pitched roofs, all in pristine condition. You expect to see a sign with the name of the museum, but these are private homes. Jeremiah Hutchinson moved to Bath in the winter of 1781 with his wife and twelve children. As you might imagine, it took two sleighs to bring them.

There's no place to stop safely, but look as you pass, at this family village of extraordinarily well-preserved Federal-style homes, unlike any other in the state.

Just south of Lisbon, on the east side of the road, is another group of historic homes, although of a much different sort. Early mills frequently provided housing for their workers, whose wages were often too low for them to afford adequate housing on their own. The *company houses* were built in rows, all alike. Most of the houses are long gone elsewhere, but eleven of them stand here in their original row.

Lisbon offers another view of the state, one that you have glimpsed from the hardscrabble farms on the back roads. This is a town with lots of guts and little money, but every year it looks just a little bit more prosperous—another house freshly painted, another porch straightened. They have a Lilac Time Festival toward the end of May. A real hometown event, it has pancake breakfasts, chicken barbecue, races, a golf tournament, quilt show, flea market, crafts, bands, singers, and a Saturday night dance. It's a time of year when summer attractions haven't opened and only the savvy traveler knows it to be a lovely and uncrowded season for a visit. For this year's dates and schedule, write the Lisbon Chamber of Commerce, Lisbon 03585 or call (603) 838–6336.

PLACES TO STAY
IN THE WESTERN WHITE MOUNTAINS
(ALL AREA CODES 603)

FRANCONIA
Bungay Jar, Easton Valley Road, 03580; 823-7775. Gardens, sauna, balconies, fireplaces at $65–$130 for a double.

Lovett's Inn by Lafayette Brook, Route 18, 03580; 823-7761. A National Register property restored as a B&B, with an eclectic dining room that serves dinner to the public at a fixed price of $35.

BETHLEHEM
The Mulburn Inn, Main Street, 03574; 869-3389 or (800) 457-9440. The former Woolworth Estate, filled with architectural details including fine woods, curved window glass, and an art deco bathroom, at rates of $60–$85.

The Little Guest House, Prospect Street, 03574; 869-5725. A cottage furnished in locally built reproductions and decorated with the owner's landscape paintings; rates begin at $60, including breakfast.

The Grand Victorian Cottage, Berkley Street, 03574; 869-5755. Grand it is, with ten guest rooms decorated in antiques. Some have private baths; rates $75–$90.

PLACES TO EAT
IN THE WESTERN WHITE MOUNTAINS
(ALL AREA CODES 603)

SUGAR HILL
Polly's Pancake Parlor, Route 117, 823-5575. Fresh made and served with real maple syrup, pancakes are served from 7:00 A.M. to 3:00 P.M. on weekdays, 7:00 A.M. to 7:00 P.M. weekends.

FRANCONIA
Franconia Inn, Easton Road, 823-5542. Well-prepared dishes, usually including trout, at $12–$18. Breakfast is served too.

BETHLEHEM
Rosa Flamingo's, Main Street, 869-3111. Contemporary restaurant with outdoor cafe in good weather, and a varied menu.

LITTLETON

Italian Oasis, 127 Main Street,
444–6995. Italian food, with an
outdoor patio in the summer,
connected to a brewpub and
microbrewery. Traditional Italian
dishes are $5.00–$13.00.

Littleton Diner, Main Street,
444–3994. The really old kind,
before stainless steel streamlined
their look, right in the center of
town.

The North Country

The north country isn't for everyone. The nearest mall is hours away; if the local grocery-store-cum-tackle-and-bait shop doesn't have it, you won't need it here. Nightlife consists of swapping fishing or birding stories in front of the fire or soothing muscles tired from canoeing, hiking, or skiing. If there is a Jacuzzi in this part of New Hampshire, it's well hidden.

But if the sight of a moose with a full rack of antlers drinking from a pool at the side of the road makes your heart beat faster, and if the cry of a loon is your favorite song, this is your Serengeti. You'll meet people here with character, not the "ayuh" and hayseed-style characters, but the real stuff. There is a ready wit born of the sense of humor necessary to those who choose the backwoods as a home. It's tent-and-canoe country, with a few fine lodgings for those who prefer their adventures to end in time for a full-course dinner.

Route 3 stays close to the Connecticut River, which at Stewartstown ceases to be the border between New Hampshire and Vermont. Travelers who have seen the Connecticut River flowing through southern New England will hardly recognize this meandering little brook as the same river. Just north of Stewartstown is a sign marking the crossing of the 45th Parallel. From that point north you are closer to the North Pole than to the equator.

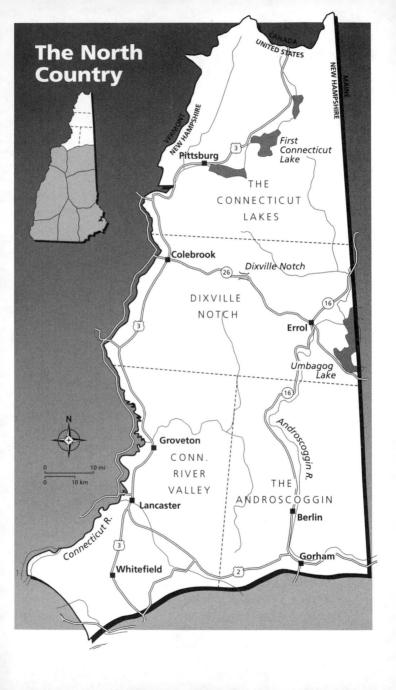

The North Country

THE
CONNECTICUT
LAKES

First Connecticut Lake

CANADA
UNITED STATES

VERMONT
NEW HAMPSHIRE

NEW HAMPSHIRE
MAINE

Pittsburg

Colebrook

Dixville Notch

DIXVILLE
NOTCH

Errol

Umbagog Lake

Androscoggin R.

N

0   10 mi
0   10 km

Groveton

CONN.
RIVER
VALLEY

THE
ANDROSCOGGIN

Lancaster

Berlin

Connecticut R.

Gorham

Whitefield

THE NORTH COUNTRY'S TOP PICKS

The Spalding Inn
Mount Prospect
Nash Stream Watershed
Pond Brook Falls
The Foolish Frog
Coon Brook Valley
Garfield Falls
Scott Bog and East Inlet
Fourth Connecticut Lake
The Glen
Beaver Brook Falls
The Balsams
Table Rock
The Flume
Huntington Cascades
Umbagog Lake Campground
Thirteen Mile Woods
Stone cairns
Holy Resurrection Church
Moose Brook State Park
Gorham Railway Station
Moose tours

Connecticut River Valley

No New England golf course has a finer view than the panorama of the White Mountains that spreads out before the greens at the **Mountain View Golf and Country Club.** Overlooking the course from the other side is the vast façade of the Mountain View Hotel, among the last of the big White Mountain resorts. The hotel is empty now and seriously in need of work, but still standing tall, like a dowager who's had to sell her pearls.

Across the street, the clubhouse of the golf course serves lunches daily from 11:00 A.M. to 4:00 P.M. Daily and weekly memberships are offered for the pool, golf course, and tennis courts. Open from May through foliage season, on Mountain View Road in Whitefield; call (603) 837–3885.

A bit farther on down Mountain View Road, *The Spalding Inn* is at once elegant and informal. First opened in 1926 on the site of an earlier hotel, the inn accommodates guests in the main lodge and in cottages near the pool and tennis courts and in a converted carriage house that was once part of the original hotel. The inn also boasts a fine bowling green; they'll show you how to play. Special arrangements allow guests to use the adjacent Mountain View golf course. The dining room menu changes nightly and might include the inn's hallmark dish, Duck Bombay. Be sure to mention any special diet, since the chef is especially creative in designing alternatives, both at breakfast and dinner. Birders will find binoculars and field guides handy by the terrace window and will enjoy the bird photographs

AUTHORS' FAVORITE ATTRACTIONS/EVENTS IN THE NORTH COUNTRY

Beaver Brook Falls, *Colebrook*

The Balsams, *Dixville Notch (603) 255–3400, (800) 255–0800 in New Hampshire, (800) 255–0600 elsewhere*

Carriage and sleigh collection at Six-Gun City, *Jefferson (603) 586–4592*

Old Time Fiddlers' Contest, *late June, Stark (603) 636–1325*

North Country Moose Festival, *late August, Pittsburgh (603) 237–8216*

Lancaster Fair, *early September, Lancaster (603) 837–2770*

taken by the innkeeper's daughter. Another daughter's paintings decorate the walls of the parlors and the innkeeper herself is responsible for the tasteful decor featuring her own collection of antiques. Rates begin at $99, including a full breakfast. The Spalding is on Mountain View Road, Whitefield 03598; telephone (603) 837–2572 or (800) 368–VIEW.

A short distance away on Route 116 is Jefferson, an unadorned town set along a ridge facing the mountains. Only the outbuildings remain of the Waumbek Hotel, which once dominated its crossroads, but there are still accommodations in town at *The Jefferson Inn.* A new ell has been added to the original 1896 Victorian house with its tower and wraparound porch, along with woodwork and other architectural detail that either match or fit the style of the original house.

Quilts warm most of the beds, and antiques are mixed with more recent furnishings, creating a nice balance of comfort and style. Families will enjoy the inn's suites

The Lost Virgin

In 1759, after repeated Indian raids from Canada had left New Hampshire farms and villages in flames, Robert Rogers of Dunbarton led a group of his famous Rangers on a raid on the village of St. Francis, home of a group of Indians converted to Catholicism by the French, who encouraged these raids by paying a bounty on white scalps during the French and Indian Wars. The Indians were busy celebrating their most recent raid when the Rangers attacked, killing and scattering the Indians. Leaving, they carried with them a pair of candlesticks and a large silver image of the Virgin Mary from the church, rich from ransomed captive settlers.

On their return, the party was forced to break up to avoid their pursuers, and the group with the Virgin, trying to cross over Jefferson Notch, floundered in the thick forests and rough terrain of the Israel River. Searches for the treasure were fruitless, and were abandoned until the gold candlesticks carried by another band turned up on the shores of Lake Memphremagog in 1816. The silver Virgin is still missing, although tales of her appearing aglow in the night to lost hunters in the area abound. Keep a sharp lookout for the statue in the Jefferson Notch area, but don't get lost in the still-thick woods.

and ample recreation space, as well as the two sociable horses in the barn. Couples will find cozy rooms stylishly decorated by the energetic new owners, who have added a historical theme and their personal art collection. The delicious European breakfast dishes have to compete with the birds outside the window for your attention. More than twenty-five species visit there, including indigo buntings. Reasonably priced, the inn is open all year except for April and November. Write The Jefferson Inn, Route 2, Jefferson 03583 or call (603) 586–7998 or (800) 729–7908.

Just before reaching Lancaster, Route 2 passes over a shoulder of **Mount Prospect,** a low peak easily spotted because of the stone tower at its summit. The tower and the stone-and-stucco "lodge" beside it were built by a man to whom the north country and everyone who travels there owes a tremendous debt. John Wingate Weeks was a U.S. senator and cabinet member to two presidents, but is remembered most as the father of the White Mountain National Forest. It was the "Weeks Law" that authorized the government to buy and preserve forest areas in the east.

The tower and buildings are now in a state park encompassing 420 acres on the mountain. The lodge contains an outstanding collection of local birds, historical displays on the White Mountains, and a gallery of photographs that reflect Mr. Weeks's prominent role in world affairs and the friends who visited the estate. Free lectures on historical and ecological topics are held at the lodge on Thursday evenings throughout the summer. The lodge and tower are open from 10:00 A.M. to 6:00 P.M. Tuesday through Sunday from mid-June until Labor Day; from Memorial Day until mid-June and Labor Day through mid-October, they are open weekends only. For a current schedule of evening programs call (603) 788–4004 or 788–3155.

Just north of the park is Lancaster, county seat of Coos County, where descendants of its original settlers, who came in 1764, still live. Lancaster has completed its section of the **New Hampshire Heritage Trail**, which will one day provide walkers with a route from the Canadian to the Massachusetts borders. The 15 miles through Lancaster are not only complete, but they have a free brochure mapping its route and describing the historic houses along the way through the center of the town. One of the buildings it points out is the Stone House on Main Street, once the only granite house in the state, and built from a single boulder (there went another glacial erratic) in 1836.

Also on the route, and on yours as well, is the **Wilder-Holton House,** the first two-storied house in the North Country, built in 1780, on the National Register and now the Historical Society Museum. Inside, along with fascinating information on the bizarre story of the Brunswick Springs Hotel (sorry, it's just over the river in Vermont, so you'll have to read about it in VERMONT: OFF THE BEATEN PATH), the museum has a children's room with dolls and a sled, a closet filled with vintage clothing, and household utensils including a hand-operated vacuum cleaner. Every alternate Sunday from the end of June until the end of September, a flea market is held on the lawn, where you can sometimes find amazing bargains. The house is open on flea market days and other times by appointment; call (603) 788–2073.

Farther north, just before Route 3 reaches Groveton, Route 110 branches to the right (east) and travels along the upper Ammonoosuc River. To the north lies the **Nash Stream Watershed,** an area whose future has been the subject of an intense battle among land developers, the state, and several conservation groups. Forty thousand acres of it have finally been secured as public lands, a mixed habitat for hawks, falcons, and smaller birds in a forested valley. Access is via Emerson Road, about 2 miles east of Groveton. Follow it another 2 miles to a fork, and then go left. After about 4.5 miles of dirt road, a right fork leads uphill to Little Pond Bog, a fine spot for fly fishing high above the valley. In the winter this area is crisscrossed by cross-country ski trails.

If you continue straight ahead less than half a mile instead of taking the right, you come to *Pond Brook Falls,* a series of waterfalls known to very few people outside of Groveton and Stark. Just after crossing a culvert you will see a pull-out area to the right. Park there and follow the trail a short distance to the lower falls (watch for moose tracks—this is a favorite path for them, too). You'll hear the falls before you see them, and then you'll see only part of them. Continuing uphill, the path ends at a second falls; from here the best route is over the sloping granite ledge alongside the rushing water. Except during spring runoff, there is plenty of room on this 50-foot-wide span of rock for both you and the brook.

Keep going upstream for an ever-changing series of falls, some gushing through narrow chutes and others spread in a filmy veil across a wide ledge. As you reach the top of each, you look up to see another of different size and shape. This is New Hampshire's sampler of waterfall styles. *Do be careful* after a rain or in the early spring when the rocks are wet, since they can be quite slippery to climb. On wet days, go through the woods next to the falls where the footing is more secure.

Back on Route 110, continue on to visit Stark, a mountain town clustered around its covered bridge under Devil's Slide, a 700-foot precipice. During World War II, Stark housed a *camp for German prisoners of war.* The remarkable story of how these men, taken prisoner in North Africa, became friends of local farmers during their long winters together is told in *Stark Decency* by Allen Koop. East of the village, on Route 110, a state sign marks the site of the camp, where only cellar holes remain.

The well-kept house with a terrace overlooking the river, just over the covered bridge in Stark, is the *Stark Village Inn Bed and Breakfast,* offering three antiques-furnished guest rooms and a great deal of homey comfort to travelers. Hiking, canoeing, fishing, climbing, cross-country skiing, and bicycling begin at the doorstep of this restored farmhouse, and photographers could spend the day sitting on the front porch capturing the river and the bridge in all their different moods and lights. A full country breakfast is cooked on the big black woodstove in the kitchen; in summer guests can eat on the terrace overlooking the river. Low rates make this a bargain as well as a treat. Write to them at R.F.D. 1, Box 389, Groveton 03582 or call (603) 636–2644.

Rock hounds take note: At Diamond Ledge on Long Mountain and also on the south slope of Percy Peak, about 200 feet below the summit, amethyst is found in the surface rock; topaz is also found at Diamond Ledge. You will need to get thorough directions locally or use a topographic map.

On the last Sunday of each June, dozens of fiddlers gather in Stark for the *Old Time Fiddlers Contest* at Whitcomb Field. Bring the whole family, lawn chairs, and a picnic lunch or buy your lunch there. Admission is charged. Call (603) 636–1325 for details.

Between the towns of Stratford and North Stratford, on the right, look for *The Foolish Frog*. This unexpected roadside museum is the personal twenty-five-year collection of Carol Hawley and Francis McMilleon, housing hundreds upon hundreds of frogs made of every conceivable material and in every imaginable style. Along with frog whatsits and gimcracks there are fine folk art sculptures including an Indonesian frog deity, a frog flute from Colombia, a rubber frog from the Amazon, plus pottery, baskets, puzzles, bottle stoppers, batiks, mechanical banks, puppets, and potholders. It is fascinating to see how a creature common throughout the world has been adapted as a design motif in so many ways. A small shelf in the center of the room displays frogs for sale, including several unique wooden toys. There is no admission charge, but there is a discreet little box for donations, which help to keep the collection growing. The Foolish Frog is open from May through foliage season, but there are no set hours. Write RR#1, Box 428, Route 3, North Stratford 03590 or call (603) 636–1887.

The Connecticut Lakes

The town of Pittsburg is geographically the largest in New Hampshire, over 20 miles wide and covering more than 360 square miles. The entire tip of New Hampshire, from the Maine to Vermont borders to the international border with Canada, lies within its boundaries. The whole town was an independent nation for three years beginning in 1832. Claimed by both New Hampshire and Canada, and with no decisive action taken by either to settle the issue, the Indian Stream Territory was left in chronic limbo. Tiring of this, and not wishing to be governed by either contender, the citizens voted their independence at a town meeting. This finally brought them to everyone's attention. After three years and a few altercations among the local militia, a Canadian sheriff's posse, and a small company of New Hampshire militia, the Republic of Indian Stream became the town of Pittsburg.

Within Pittsburg's borders lie all four of the Connecticut Lakes and Lake Francis, and mile after mile of forests, mountain streams, bogs, and assorted wilderness lands. Pittsburg's main (almost its only) road borders each lake in turn until it finally climbs the "height-of-land" to the Canadian border station. ("Height-of-land" is a term commonly used in the north country to describe the high point of any of the area's many ridges.) At nearly any point you may see deer or moose by the roadside.

What is unique here is the series of pristine water bodies. Uninhabited by man, these provide habitat for wild shorebirds found in few other places. Loon populations are increasing here. You can put in a canoe on nearly any pond, and you are welcome to roam over the woods roads built by the timber companies as long as they are not barred. The whole area abounds with trout.

Coon Brook Valley, a long, wide, marshy area cut by a woods road, is a sure place to see moose at almost any time of day. To find it, look for a road marked MAGALLOWAY TOWER entering Route 3 from the right. Go a

Coon Brook Valley

few yards north and take the road entering from the opposite side of Route 3. Just drive in and park in an open spot—you may even see moose before you park.

For an adventure into the outer reaches of the wilderness, but one that requires only a short hike, search out *Garfield Falls.* Take the above-mentioned gravel road marked MAGALLOWAY TOWER, following the tower signs until you reach the height of land. At this point a dirt road to the tower goes off to the right, but you should keep going. About 2 miles after you pass Paradise Camp on your left, you will go down a hill and see a road bearing off to the right (the road straight ahead of you may be blocked just below this). Follow the road to the right $1\frac{1}{10}$ mile to where it makes a sharp left turn and crosses a bridge. Take the dirt road right at the turn.

It's narrow, but unless there have been heavy rains, it is easily passable without four-wheel drive. In another $1^1/_{10}$ mile the road opens out into a yard (an open area where logs are stored). Park there and follow the trail into the woods on the left side of the road. It may take a minute to find it if there have been logging operations there recently, but it is close by a tumble of large rocks.

Garfield Falls is only a five-minute walk from here, through a forest carpeted in the spring with trillium, clintonia, bunchberry, wood sorrel, and occasional moose droppings that look like piles of nutmegs beside (or in) the trail. The falls will be to your left, dropping off the facing side of a chasm into a pool almost directly under your feet. It comes through a zigzag chute and then bounces off the boulder with such force that it has worn a depression in the face of the cliff as well as a cave at its base where its velocity creates a whirlpool. Below the falls the river is split by a giant boulder from which you can get an excellent view of the falls—and the deeply undercut bank that you were just standing on!

This is not a trip to begin with bald tires, with a near-empty gas tank, or in a downpour of rain, but it is quite an easy one. The distances aren't great, just slow to cover. Before you curse the timber companies for their cutting throughout this area, remember two points. First, you are traveling on their roads, which are the only access to these areas in case of forest fires. Second, their cutting, done with the techniques that they now employ, creates a far more inviting habitat for birds and animals than dense forest provides.

A little farther up Route 3, just above Second Connecticut Lake, another timber road to the right leads to **Scott Bog and East Inlet.** The road curves down into a valley and across a stream to a rough T, where you should go left to find Scott Bog or right to find East Inlet. The latter is a former log drive impoundment from which logs were floated out on the spring thaw. In 1987, Champion Paper Company donated 426 acres of pristine pond and moose pasture here, including a tract of virgin spruce and fir, to the Nature Conservancy. The Scott Bog-East Inlet area is considered by birders to offer the best sightings in the north country, with spruce grouse, Canada jay, sixteen warbler varieties, and the rare black-backed wood-pecker. Sightings of eighty to ninety species in three days are quite common here.

Wandering around on these woods roads is a lot easier and less nerve-wracking with the inexpensive map "Roads and Trails, Connecticut Lake Region" printed on waterproof paper and available at most stores in the area.

The Connecticut River, barely a trickle now, crosses the road above Second Connecticut Lake, and the tiny **Deer Mountain Campground** sits on its northern banks. Its twenty campsites are rustic: No hot showers, flush toilets, or camp store here, but there is plenty of quiet and the riverbanks are alive with birds. The **Moose Falls Flowage,** just north of the campground, is a good place to put in a canoe. The campground is open from May until the end of October.

Third Connecticut Lake has a boat ramp right off Route 3, but **Fourth Connecticut Lake** takes a bit more effort. Only about an acre in size, it is reached by a trail from the U.S. Customs station at the Canadian border. The trail, which is actually the cleared swath along the border, is "steep and rugged," as the map warns. Because it is rocky, it is not a hike for street shoes. Park and sign in at the customs station, where they will give you a trail map. It is only about ½ mile to the seventy-five–acre site that Champion Paper Company donated to the Nature Conservancy in 1990. Be sure to walk around the upper part of the lake to find the spot where the first few drops of the mighty Connecticut River trickle from the rocks.

The best way to enjoy this area is to settle in for a few days, and the best place to do that is in a comfortable log cabin or lodge overlooking a lake. **The Glen,** a former private estate, looks as though it had grown there with the tall spruce trees that line the shores of First Connecticut Lake. The big lodge, which has been welcoming guests for more than thirty years, is a convivial place with a huge stone fireplace and comfortable Adirondack log and maple furniture; you can also opt for the seclusion of your own cabin. The atmosphere here is comfortable, not cute. There are no frilly curtains or designer sheets, but you won't be roughing it either.

All meals are included in the rate, and they'll pack you a box lunch; they will even fill your thermos with hot coffee when you leave for your day's adventure. Dinners in the dining room are generous, including such entrees as haddock filet with shrimps and scallops, served with vegetables, pilaf, and wine. The whipped cream on your chocolate cream pie is real, and the vegetables in the salad bar are crisp and fresh. Meals prepared to suit special diets are treated with the same careful attention. But you can expect one distraction while you're eating: The birdfeeders outside the dining room windows are aswarm with hummingbirds.

The tone and warmth of The Glen is set by its owner, Betty Falton. She helps guests choose places to hike, fish, bird, or just wander around, suggesting routes and telling about her own favorite nooks and crannies. Betty keeps rental boats moored on various lakes so you won't have to haul them around, or you can bring your own. She loves her "neighborhood," but she stresses that this is not the place for everyone's taste. "If you can't walk to the brook without seeing something interesting, you don't belong here," she is quick to tell prospective guests.

When the full moon rises over Mount Magalloway, reflecting in the lake and outlining the spiky silhouettes of the fir trees around the lake, it looks like the stage set for *Rose Marie*. If the lure of the wilderness charms you, there's no finer place to enjoy it. The Glen is open from mid-May to October, when you can call for reservations at (603) 538-6500. From December to April call Betty at (508) 475-0559, or call (800) 445-GLEN.

South of Pittsburg you have a choice of roads. Route 145 covers the same route, but in a straighter line. At least on the map it's straighter—if you ironed out the hills, the length would probably be the same. The view from the hilltops, past hillside farms and forests to the skyline of mountains to the south, makes it a nice change from Route 3's river-bottom route.

Beaver Brook Falls drops almost onto Route 145, about 2 ½ miles before you reach Colebrook. You will see small parking areas on both sides of the road before you see the falls. Be prepared for a surprise, especially if it has rained recently—somehow one doesn't expect the 35-foot straight drop of a waterfall to appear out of the woods, particularly on the side of the road. Below, a series of cascades spill from pool to pool. At the foot of the falls is a small park with picnic tables and a swimming hole. If you aren't going into the tip of the state, you can get to the falls via Route 145 out of Colebrook (the sign is marked CLARKSVILLE), making the 5-mile side trip before going on to Dixville Notch.

Dixville Notch

*U*nlike most of New Hampshire's other notches, which run north and south, Dixville lies east and west. Route 26 follows the Mohawk River all the way from Colebrook to the notch itself. About 3 miles outside of Colebrook, look for East Colebrook Road going up the hill to your left. The road continues upward giving fine views over the notch. At the intersection by an old schoolhouse, a left will bring you to a unique lodging, ***Rooms with a View.*** Unlike most New Hampshire bed and breakfasts, this one is in a newly-built home, set in a hilltop meadow with its porch rockers overlooking the Connecticut Valley and Dixville Notch. The kitchen is in the center of the house, and you are welcome to watch Sonja bake her bread (fresh every day and sweetened with her own honey) in the huge Tulikivi soapstone stove that dominates the room. Or you can just sit in the bright dining room and enjoy the view while she serves you a full, made-from-scratch country breakfast.

Each room is different, with a graceful mix of antique and new furniture. Beds are warmed by quilts pieced by Sonja, and each bathroom has a fuzzy, thick sheepskin mat. The house was built to share, and it's a warm and welcoming place to come home to after your north

Authors' Note

*W*e arrived at The Balsams right after a heavy thunderstorm, when the wind howled through Dixville Notch and rain pelted us in a brief but violent torrent. The sun had come out as we pulled up, and in front of the hotel we found an assemblage of bellmen, waiters, housekeeping staff, one of the owners and several guests, all looking anxiously at the cliffs behind the hotel. One of the bellmen left the group to help us unload but kept looking upward, attentive and hospitable as ever, but clearly preoccupied. More people came out of the hotel—the head of guest services, a couple more waiters, and two men in tennis whites, all looking intently up at the cliff.

"Is something the matter?" we finally asked.

"Oh, yes," the bellman answered anxiously, squinting up at the cliff again. "The Peregrine falcons have a nest up there and we're afraid that the storm may have dislodged it or hurt the fledglings." Only at The Balsams would the world virtually stop for a nest of rare birds.

country travels. Moderately priced and open year-round, for reservations write Rooms with a View, R. R. #1, Forbes Road, Colebrook 03576 or call (603) 237–5106 or (800) 499–5106.

For many visitors, the goal and the reward of the long trip to this far-off tip of the state is staying at the world-class grand hotel set just below the head of the notch. *The Balsams* is unique in so many ways that we'll mention only a few. Once one of many large resort hotels where city families came to spend the summer before the days of air conditioning, The Balsams is still thriving, having weathered the tough financial climates as well as it has weathered its natural climate. It has turned the harsh winters to advantage by opening a family ski area and miles of cross-country ski trails, keeping Lake Gloriette open for skating, giving snowshoe lessons, and offering the free use of snowshoes.

Their success is even more surprising because of the hotel's remote location, but therein lies another unique feature. Unlike the other big hotels that were built in the busy White Mountain circuit, The Balsams stands alone, with none of the tourist attractions of the more heavily traveled routes. It is a gracious and highly civilized oasis in a vast wilderness, and its owners have turned that fact to their advantage. They have provided so many activities, sporting opportunities, social events, and gastronomic pleasures that it would take a week to enjoy them all. In the summer, there are golf, hiking, walks with a staff naturalist, fishing in the lakes and streams, boating, canoeing, tennis, moose watching, swimming, dancing, movies, cooking lessons, a daily sports program, and the opportunity just to sit on the wide veranda and look at the mountains.

One of the few resorts operating on the American plan, The Balsams includes all meals in the room rate, and you won't want to miss one. Breakfast and lunch are offered as buffets with service, and always make for an impressive production rich in variety. Lunch brings an entire table of mouth-watering desserts, of which you are welcome to sample as many as your appetite allows. Dinner is more formal, with a wide choice of entrees as elegant and innovative or as traditional as you like. A sauté of scallops and shrimp with ginger and cilantro, veal Oscar, broiled tuna with a citrus butter sauce, venison loin with wild mushrooms, or pecan roasted pork may be among the several nightly choices. This is not the usual hotel dining room fare, and this top-quality cuisine is one of the primary reasons for the success of the entire resort. Another reason is the warm and personal service in the dining room and elsewhere in the hotel.

Did we mention that The Balsams welcomes families and provides special activities, ski programs, and babysitting so that parents can enjoy some time to themselves as well? While there, don't miss *The Apple Tree,* a shop featuring locally made products, books, and quality gifts. Or the room where the residents of Dixville gather every four years at midnight to cast the nation's first ballots for the presidential election. Write The Balsams, Dixville Notch 03576; call (603) 255–3400 or (800) 255–0800 in New Hampshire or (800) 255–0600 elsewhere.

Between meals at The Balsams, explore the notch. You can vary your level of exercise, beginning with a walk around the Lake Gloriette walking trail, a 1.4-mile loop, with the hotel's *Natural History Handbook* as your guide. This informative little book explains the geology of the notch and helps you identify its abundant wildflowers and birds. More energy is required for the climb up to *Table Rock,* especially if you take the rock-strewn trail that goes almost straight up from the notch. A more gentle ascent can be made by a trail beginning near the Balsam/Wilderness Ski Area entrance road. Table Rock overlooks The Balsams, the lake, and the notch, but it's no place for an acrophobic.

At the point where the trail drops steeply to Table Rock, another trail leads away from the ledges. If you follow it for a few yards you will come to a deep split in the rock face. This *Ice Chasm* has snow and ice in it even during the hottest summer days. Although there is no sign leading to it, you won't have trouble finding it; you just have to know it is there. *Be careful:* It can be dangerous if you get too close to the sharp edge. A new trail in progress from Huntington Cascades to Table Rock makes a complete circuit through the notch opening up new views.

After hiking, be sure to stop for a refreshing drink of pure mountain spring water at the newly built *Spring House,* an exact reproduction of the original, which was a popular destination for a Sunday "drive." Many locals remember the spring as the scene of their first kiss or even the place of their marriage proposal. There must be something about the water!

If you want to know where to buy hand-tied flies, hire a good fishing guide, find Mable Sims's fish pond, or rent a canoe, ask Ray Gorman, the chief concierge at The Balsams. He's an experienced outdoorsman and a native of the area, the perfect concierge for such a resort. He can also tell you about the "lonesome loon" in the lake.

The Flume is on the other side of the notch, and on your way there you can appreciate how wild this notch is compared to Franconia, Pinkham, and even Crawford notches. It's a *real* notch, where you go over a hump in the road, through a cleft in the cliffs, and down a steep, winding road squeezed between two tree-covered walls. The difference is geological: The surface rock here has been tilted on end so that its strata stand upright, causing the craggy eroded points of rock that give it such a wild aspect.

About a mile past the head of the notch look for a picnic area on the left. The geology changes back to granite here, as Flume Brook carves a gorge more than 200 feet long with sides so straight it almost seems to have been built from cut blocks of stone. It is 40 feet deep in places, as the brook drops from pool to pool and finally over the edge of a ledge. Walk along the rim, and in the spring look for trillium and white and pink lady's slippers beside the trail. They are protected species, so enjoy them in place.

Just a few yards down Route 26, this time on the right, is the road to a second picnic area. **Huntington Cascades** is reached by a short path to the brook and then a short walk upstream. The falls continue above the one that you can see from the base, but there is no trail up the steep slope beside the falls, so most visitors simply enjoy the lower section as it rushes in its curving path over the rocks. If you do go exploring here, be careful and stay away from the edge, which has been undercut by the brook. In case you wondered, the little cemetery by the entrance to the parking area contains the remains of some of the area's earliest settlers.

The 5 miles of road between Huntington Cascades and the town of Errol is a prime stretch for moose viewing, so drive slowly and keep watch. You can't miss the Errol International Airport, whose building is so tiny that its long name has to be abbreviated to fit across its façade.

Each of the two roads leaving from the far end of Errol's main street will take you to the Maine border. Route 16, to the left, offers a pleasant drive along the upper Androscoggin and the Magalloway rivers. Route 26 leads to the southern shores of *Lake Umbagog* and one of the most beautiful and unusual campgrounds in all of New England.

Lake Umbagog is a wildlife sanctuary, with one of the nation's largest loon nesting areas. Bald eagles have also nested there for several years, raising chicks of their own and even a chick from an adopted egg from New York State. Other bird life and, of course, moose abound. *Umbagog Lake Campground* is, like most of this north country, not for everyone. "We cater to canvas," says owner Jim Willard, by which he means that they will accommodate your RV if they have room, but the campground is really designed for tents. Along with sites overlooking the length of Umbagog's blue waters, the shady wooded sites and the handful of cottages, there are more than thirty wilderness campsites on islands or shores of the lake without road access. The farthest of these is 11 miles from the campground; Jim will take you to your site by motorboat if you don't want to paddle all the way. You can bring your own rowboat or canoe, or rent theirs, for exploring the lake.

These sites are isolated, at least a half-mile apart, some on islands. They are not for beginning campers, but for the woodswise and the waterwise they offer real camping that is very hard to find. Open from Memorial Day to mid-September; you can reserve sites. Write Umbagog Lake Campground, P.O. Box 181, Errol 03579; call (603) 482–7795.

In Errol, *Saco Bound* rents canoes and kayaks, as well as operating a full transportation service so you can put in at

A Note about Our Less Appealing Wildlife

While May's lilacs are safe as the state's flower, there is talk every spring about changing the state bird from the purple finch (which we rarely see) to the mosquito or blackfly, which we see all too often. Unless you have allergies to their bites, these springtime insects are merely an annoyance. They don't carry malaria or yellow fever as their tropical relatives do, and slapping them is a source of moderate exercise.

But in the north country, especially in May and June, it is wise to be prepared with long sleeves, long pants, and shirts with collars when these voracious creatures are at their worst— evenings and mornings and in the deep woods.

Everyone has a favorite brand of repellent; we favor Natrapel for most places, the only repellent we know of with EPA approval that comes with a propellant-free spray and a recyclable bottle. Natrapel is a New Hampshire product, created by people who know mosquitos and black flies intimately. For sources call (800) 258-4696 or write Tender Corp., P.O. Box 290, Littleton 03561.

one place and be picked up at a different location. In the summer they offer reasonably priced guided day trips complete with a barbecue lunch. They operate a whitewater canoe and kayak school at Errol, as well as a campground for their customers. Write Saco Bound, Box 119, Center Conway 03813; call (603) 447–2177 or 447–3801.

The Androscoggin

S outh of Errol on Route 16 begins a scenic stretch where the road and the Androscoggin River travel side by side through ***Thirteen Mile Woods.*** The river is wide and for the most part gentle, and there are put-ins at several different points. If you have ever held a paddle, you will long to be on the water in this flat reach where the trees overhang the water. There is even a campground, the Mollidgewock, right on the river and designed primarily for canoeists. It is open from mid-May to December 1. Be sure to call them at (603) 482–3373 to reserve a site, since its half-mile frontage on calm water and rapids is a favorite teaching area for groups learning whitewater techniques.

Motorists will find good places for a riverside picnic, or to just sit and watch the river traffic go by. Below the Thirteen Mile Woods is another area frequented by moose, where it is not unusual to see them beside (or in) the road.

North of Berlin look for the **stone cairns** in the river, among the last reminders of the days of the logging drives that were common in this country during the nineteenth and early twentieth centuries. These mid-river cairns served as the point from which the great chain booms were secured. These captured and held a vast flotilla of logs during the annual spring release of the timber that had been harvested during the winter. As trees were cut during the winter, the logs were hauled into impoundment ponds. During the runoff, the dams holding these ponds were released. The water and logs in it broke into a wild frenzy of energy and wood that found its way downstream into the sawmills and paper plants of New England.

Berlin (pronounced with the accent on the first syllable) is a paper mill town; you can't miss the smokestacks of the James River Corporation. It has been a paper town

Holy Resurrection Chuch

ever since the first logging camp was established in 1825, although the first paper mill didn't open until 1852. At one time, it was estimated that the paper produced in Berlin annually would cover a road 15 feet wide that would run nineteen times around the world. The mill brought immigrants from Canada and as far away as Russia. These ethnic groups have mixed and moved, but a few traces remain from the days when church services in the community were conducted in five different languages.

Saint Anne's church, a classic French-Canadian brick structure, rises like a fortress in the center of town, enormously tall, with an oversized statue on top. But far more unexpected is **Holy Resurrection Church.** Take Mount Forist Street, which intersects with Main Street near the post office, and follow it up the hill. When we say *up*, we mean almost straight up what may well be New Hampshire's steepest street. Just before the street ends, go left on Russian Street, still going uphill, and look to your right. Six polished, gold-leafed, onion-shaped domes crown a gem of a Russian Orthodox church on the corner of Petrograd Street. Each dome is surmounted by a double patriarchal gold cross; the rest of the church is white. It sits above the city overlooking the smokestacks and rows of company housing below, a poignant and rare reminder of the homesickness of the many peoples that were propelled into this strange and new land.

For a fine view over the mountains to the west, take the *Cates Hill Scenic Route,* turning right off High Street onto Hillside Avenue. The road continues to climb until it reaches a ridge of cleared meadows with a backdrop of mountains. You can reach Hillside Avenue from Route 16 north of town by taking the road marked "Coos County Home" and continuing to the top of the hill.

On Jimtown Road, just off Route 5 west of Gorham, is a very pleasant campground at *Moose Brook State Park.* Its forty-six sites are well spaced in open forest, with a few at the edge of a field. An ingenious warming pool brings the icy-cold waters of Moose Brook up to a more suitable temperature before it flows into the swimming pool downstream. There is a picnic area near the swimming pool. Be sure to notice the architecture of the administration building, which is a classic of Civilian Conservation Corps (CCC) construction. The park is open from late May through Labor Day. Call (603) 271–3628 for information.

Across from the Town Hall on the Common in Gorham, the Victorian *Railway Station* has been turned into a museum by the local historical society. The collection emphasizes the years when the railway was the lifeblood of the region, but contains other memorabilia as well, including a stereoscope visitors can actually use to view the collection of historic cards. Hours vary; call (603) 466–5570.

While in Gorham, inquire at the information booth about *moose tours* sponsored by the Chamber of Commerce. These take visitors by van to some of the most likely locations for spotting moose, showing a video about the local logging heritage on the way. The tour leaves the information booth on the common at sunset daily from mid-May through Columbus Day weekend. Call (603) 466–3103 or 752–6060.

While the Old Man of The Mountain, in Franconia Notch, is the state's best known symbol, *The Old Man of the Valley* in Shelburne is virtually unknown. This will most likely change now that a modest sign has appeared on the south side of Route 2 between Gorham and the Maine border. Park in the pull-out just east of the sign. Walk back to the sign, where a short trail enters the woods. A short distance ahead is a large stone with the profile of a man on one side. Surely, you say, this has just been sculpted to look this way, but a walk around the stone shows a jumble of perfectly natural planes that form the face when viewed from the front.

PLACES TO STAY
IN THE NORTH COUNTRY
(ALL AREA CODES 603)

JEFFERSON
Josselyn's Log Cabins, North
Road, 03583; (603) 586–4507.
Real log cabins sleep four to ten
and have full kitchens; priced
from $40 per couple.

Applebrook Bed and Breakfast,
Route 115A, 03583; (603)
586–7713 or (800) 545–6504.

PITTSBURG
Mountain View Cabins and
Campground, Route 3, 03592;
(603) 538–6305. Log cabins open
year-round, located on the main
snowmobile trail system. All
have central heat, some with
fireplaces or wood stoves, too.

Magalloway Cabins, First
Connecticut Lake, 03592; (603)
538–6353. Housekeeping units
with baseboard heat, open all
year and convenient to
snowmobile trail system.

GORHAM
Gorham House Bed and
Breakfast, 55 Main Street, 03581;
(603) 466–2271. A stunning
Victorian "painted lady" you can't

miss as you drive through
Gorham. Period-piece rooms and
moderate rates.

Town and Country Motor Inn,
Route 2, 03581; (603) 466–3315.
Well-kept motel with swimming
pool; $50–$70 in high-season.

SHELBURNE
Philbrook Farm, 881 North Road,
03581; (603) 466–3831. A
comfortable, old-fashioned place
where families come year after
year; $110–$140, with breakfast
and dinner.

PLACES TO EAT
IN THE NORTH COUNTRY
(ALL AREA CODES 603)

GROVETON
McKenzie's Diner, Route 3, (603)
636–1404. Open every day from
5:30 A.M. to 8:00 P.M., this
restaurant serves generous
portions and hearty breakfasts at
budget prices.

WHITEFIELD
Barbara's Little Restaurant, Route
116, (603) 837–3161. Home-style
cooking in generous portions,
serving three meals a day.
Entrees $7.00–$13.00.

The Inn at Whitefield, Route 3, (603) 837–2760. Continental menu, moderately priced, adjacent to Weathervane Theatre.

LANCASTER
Lost Nation Natural Foods, Main Street, (603) 788–4141. Stop here for picnic makings, including some ready-made cold dishes.

PITTSBURG
Maria's, Route 3, (603) 538–7736. In the center of the village and open from 5:30 A.M. until 2:00 P.M., serving very good breakfasts and lunches.

Midtown Restaurant, Route 3, (603) 538–6679. In the center of Pittsburg, serving three meals a day, in generous servings.

The Glen (see chapter text) serves dinner to nonguests by reservation.

GORHAM
Yokohama Restaurant, 288 Main Street, (603) 466–2501. Pan Asian menu, with particular emphasis on Japanese food; entrees $6.00–$12.00.

Wilfred's Turkey Dinners, Main Street, (603) 466–2380. Family-run restaurant serves other standards, but the specialty is turkey; entrees are $7.00–$13.00.

BERLIN
Northland Restaurant and Dairy Bar, Riverside Drive, (603) 752–6210. Open daily for lunch and dinner, prices $8.00–$12.00.

About the Authors

Barbara Radcliffe Rogers and Stillman Rogers have, jointly and singly, written and illustrated more than twenty-five books, most of them on travel, wildlife, and gardening. Titles include *Galapagos, Safari, The Portugal Traveler, Big Cats, Giant Pandas, Natural Wonders of Vermont* and *Exploring Europe by Boat.* They have written and illustrated several books in the *Children of the World* series describing the lives and cultures of children from Argentina to Zambia. Barbara has written articles for *Yankee* Magazine, *Country Journal, Animal Kingdom,* the *Los Angeles Times*, and others, including a column, "Adventures" for *The Sunday Sentinel,* in Keene, New Hampshire. Stillman's photographs have illustrated these and other articles.

In *New Hampshire: Off The Beaten Path,* they write for the first time about their home state. Although they have explored its trails and back roads since childhood, they still find it as fascinating as the most exotic locales in their wide repertoire of travels.

Index

Interested in more New England getaways? Try these favorites from Globe Pequot:

Recommended Bed & Breakfasts: New England $16.95
The finest B&B's in Connecticut, Rhode Island, Massachusetts, Vermont, New Hampshire, and Maine.

Recommended Country Inns® New England $16.95
Discover the gracious hospitality of New England's finest inns.

Romantic Days and Nights in™ Boston $15.95
Thirty intimate escapes in the "hub."

Great Family Vacations: Northeast $14.95
Twenty-four fun-filled vacations for the entire family!

Daytrips and Getaway Weekends in New England $17.95
Put aside a few days to explore all New England has to offer.

To order these Globe Pequot books or to request a catalog, call 1-800-243-0495, fax 1-800-820-2329, or write The Globe Pequot Press, P.O. Box 833, Old Saybrook, CT 06475. Visit our Web site at http://www.globe-pequot.com.